MUSES IN EXILE

Paljor Publications
New Delhi

Also by Bhuchung D. Sonam

Dandelions of Tibet *(2002)*
Tibet: A Conflict of Duality *(forthcoming)*

MUSES IN EXILE

An Anthology of Tibetan Poetry

Edited with an Introduction by
Bhuchung D. Sonam

First Edition 2004

© 2004 Bhuchung D. Sonam
bdsonam@rediffmail.com

All rights reserved

Cover art © Sonam Dhondup, by arrangement
with Amnye Machen Institute

Designed by Tenzin Sangmo

Published by:
Paljor Publications
H-9 Jangpura Ext.
New Delhi - 14, India
www.paljorpublications.com

Printed at:
Archana
787, Church Road, Jangpura, Bhogal
New Delhi-110014
Tel.: 91-11-24311992

ISBN : 81- 86230- 48-3

for

T.C.V

Copyright Credits:

Chögyam Trungpa Rinpoche's poems are reprinted by arrangement with Shambhala Publications, Boston, USA. They are:
A Letter to Marpa, Burdensome, Tibetan Pilgrim, Season's Greetings, As Skylarks Hunt For Their Prey from *TIMELY RAIN: Selected Poetry of Chögyam Trungpa.* © 1972, 1983, 1998 by Diana J. Mukpo.
Haiku is reproduced by permission of Trident Publications, from *TIMELY RAIN: Selected Poetry of Chögyam Trungpa.* © 1972, 1983, 1998 by Diana J. Mukpo.
PAN-DHARMADOLLAR from *First Thought Best Thought: 108 Poems* by Chögyam Trungpa. © 1983 by Diana J. Mukpo.

The Monk and the Nun © Lhasang Tsering

Fresh Winds, Exile, Lines to a Prostitute, A Poet's Reply, Cold Mountain Song, Of Exile and Refuge, After Spring, Existence Anonymous, Poisons of the Mind, A Poem of Separation, Broken Tune © K. Dhondup

In Search of Gesar's Sword, First Snowfall, On the Wings, At the End of the Rainbow, Cold Frost, To You from Exile, The Weatherman, The Nomads I, II & III, The Hermit © Gyalpo Tsering

The Broken Plough, America, The Wish, To Boat People © Norbu Zangpo

Mountains, Ways of the World, Dharmakaya, I Am What I Am, Alaskans, One with Nature © Ngodup Paljor

Rainbow and a Glass Cage, Plea–(Dance of the Shadow), May Musings, Vignettes in Random, Untitled, Burlesque, Autumn Love Dance–time for reckoning, Song for a Season, Song for the Dead © Tenzing Sonam

Recollection, Zero, The Dalai Lama, Torn Between Two Countries, My Tibet, Haiku, Calendar on the Wall, Nirvana, In Case You Forgot, Made in China, and Om Mani Padme Hum from *Recollections of a Tibetan* by

Tsoltim N. Shakabpa published by Publish America © 2003 Tsoltim N. Shakabpa. Reprinted with kind permission from the author.

If I Die, Destination, I Wish To Be Buddha, Reality and Illusion, Pass By, Visions in Snippets, Let Us and Let Us Not, and untitled © *G. C.* Printed from G. C's original diary (Collection Tenzin Tsundue).

A Matter Not of Order from *In the Absent Everyday* (forthcoming); Hibernation, Third lesson, and The water song from *Rules of the House*, published by Apogee Press © 2002 Tsering Wangmo Dhompa

Exile House, Horizon, The Third Side of a Coin, The Flower and I, Ersatz Scare-crow, Spider Webbed, Looking for My Onion from *Crossing the Border* and *KORA: a story and eleven poems* © 1999, 2003 by Tenzin Tsundue. Reprinted with kind permission from the author.

Guilty in Love, Pyre of Patriotism, For Appearance and Worse, and Conflict © Topden Tsering

Mother, A Voice, Freedom, Nangsel, They are Still Too Young, Love Story of a Snail Queen, A Whisper, Destination Heart, Silent Souls, Stolen Moments of Life, Twilight's Delight, and The Mother Cuckoo © Tsamchoe Dolma

The Freedom Song, My Last Wish, Together, The Fallen Leaf, A Pledge from *Young Tibet* © 2002 by Thupten N. Chakrishar. Reprinted with kind permission from the author.

Lone-1, Dylan, Me and Robin Hood, Dandelions of Tibet, Of Death and Peace, Song of an Old Tibetan, From a Prison Diary, Gendun Choephel Wailing From Nangtse Shar Prison © Bhuchung D. Sonam

A Dry Leaf, Stone Boy's Confession, The Call from *The Call* by Namgyal Phuntsok, Thriving On Flame from *Silent Observer* by Namgyal Phuntsok © 2003, 2004 Namgyal Phuntsok. Reprinted with kind permission from the author.

India - I See It Soon Depart © Tenzin Trinley

Dreams, Romancing the Night, and Unfulfilled Promises © Tenzin Gelek

A Blind Farmer? © Ugen Choephel

Don't be Afraid Mother, Barkhor, and In This Life I Saw © Kathup Tsering

Ode to Dhondup Gyal © Kalsang Wangdue

I Have Aged © Tenzin Palzom

Caveat © Sherab W. Choephell

Is It Snowing In Tibet? © Wongchen Tsering

Cry Tibet, Emptiness Again © Gur Gyal

Emptiness © Tsering Dolkar

Shambhala © Dhargyal Tsering

The View © Pema Tenzin

Three Things I Wait For © Dawa Woeser

The Majestic Himalayas © Cherin' Norbu

Mr. Fart © Tshering Dorjee

Acknowledgement

I would like to thank my friend Tenzin Tsundue for introducing me to many of the poets featured here and for sourcing their works, for his constant support and encouragement. This book is his as much as mine. Jane Perkins and Lhasang Tsering for their guidance and making me realize my shortfalls in using the right words; Pema Yeshi of The Library of Tibetan Works and Archives for allowing me free access to library facilities, and for all the exile poets for their contribution. It is to them and the future poets that I dedicate this book. I would also like to thank all my friends who helped me along the tortuous path and for welcoming me in their rooms when the penny pinched hard — and for their belief in me. Last, but not least, I would like to thank Sharon Brown Bacon without whose kind assistance this book would not have seen the light of day.

B. D. S.

I have no name
But others call me 'The Nameless One'
How can one escape the imprisonment
And burst the chain of concept?

Chögyam Trungpa

Oh Poet! How can springtime, that already has
reached out to other men,
Still not release your
Fountain of creative energy?

Xu Zhimo

Contents

Introduction   ix

Gendun Choephel   1
Milarepa's Reply
Oh Where?
Rebkong
Manasarovar

ChögyamTrungpa   7
A Letter to Marpa
Haiku
Burdensome
Tibetan Pilgrim
Season's Greetings
As Skylarks Hunt for Their Prey
PAN-DHARMADOLLAR
Highlands of Tibet

K. Dhondup   19
Fresh Winds
Exile
Lines to a Prostitute
A Poet's Poetry
Cold Mountain Songs
Of Exile and Refuge

After Spring
Existence Anonymous
Poisons of the Mind
A Poem of Separation
Broken Tunes

Ngodup Paljor   32
Mountains
untitled
Ways of the World
Dharmakaya
I Am What I Am
Alaskans
One with Nature

Lhasang Tsering   40
The Monk and the Nun

Tsoltim N. Shakabpa   42
Recollections
Zero
The Dalai Lama
Torn Between Two Countries
Made In China
My Tibet
OM MANI PADME HUM
Haiku

Calendar on the Wall
Nirvana
In Case You Forgot

Gyalpo Tsering   53
In Search of Gesar's Sword
First Snowfall
On the Wing
Cold Frost
To You from Exile
At the End of the Rainbow
The Weatherman (Ngagpa-la)
The Nomad I
The Nomad II
The Nomad III
The Hermit

Norbu Zangpo   67
The Broken Plough
To Boat People
America
The Wish

Tenzing Sonam   71
Rainbow and a Glass Cage
Plea – (Dance of the Shadows)
May Musings

Vignettes in Random
untitled
Burlesque
Autumn Love Dance – time for reckoning
Song for the Dead
Song for a Season

Gendun Choephel (G. C.)   83
If I Die
Destination
I Wish To Be Buddha
Reality and Illusion
Pass By
Visions in Snippets
Let Us and Let Us Not
untitled

Tsering Wangmo Dhompa   92
A Matter Not of Order
The water song
Third lesson
Hibernation

Tenzin Tsundue   103
Exile House
Horizon
The Third Side of a Coin
The Flower and I

untitled
Spider-webbed
Looking For My Onion
I am a Terrorist

Topden Tsering   114
Pyre of Patriotism
Guilty in Love
For Appearance and Worse
Conflict

Tsamchoe Dolma   122
Mother
A Voice
Freedom
Nangsel
They Are Still Too Young
Love Story of the Snail Queen
A Whisper
Destination…Heart
Silent Souls
Stolen Moments of Life
Twilight's Delight
The Mother Cuckoo

Bhuchung D. Sonam   139
Lone-1
From a Prison Diary
Dylan, Me and Robin Hood

Dandelions of Tibet
Of Death and Peace
Song of an Old Tibetan
Gendun Choephel Wailing From Nangtse Shar Prison

Tenzin Trinley   149
India – I See It Soon Depart

Kalsang Wangdu   150
Ode to Dhondup Gyal

Ugen Choephel   152
A Blind Farmer?

Thupten N. Chakrishar   153
The Freedom Song
My last Wish
Together
The Fallen Leaf
A Pledge

Namgyal Phuntsok   159
A Dry Leaf
Stone Boy's Confession
The Call
Thriving in the Flames

Tenzin Palzom   163
I Have Aged

Sherab W. Choephel   164
Caveat

Anonymous   165
Tibet is My Destination

Wongchen Tsering   167
Is It Snowing In Tibet?

Gur Gyal   168
Cry   Tibet
Emptiness Again

Tsering Dolkar   169
Emptiness

Dhargyal Tsering   171
Shambhala

Pema Tenzin   172
The View

Dawa Woeser   173
Three Things I Wait For…

Kathup Tsering   174
Don't be Afraid Mother
Barkhor
In This Life I Saw

Cherin' Norbu   179
The Majestic Himalayas

Tenzin Gelek   180
Dreams
Romancing the Night
Unfulfilled Promises

Tsering Dorjee   183
Mr. Fart

Introduction

Exile is the shifting sands of hope mingled with the crippling sorrow of estrangement. When hope fades into the distant horizon, and only the pangs of displacement remain, exile becomes a hollow existence hanging upon a thin thread of moral courage. Exile is, in many ways, an opportunity and a severe test of communal fortitude. Inspite of upheavals and separations, deaths and destruction in our homeland, we have withstood this testing period and emerged enriched.

In the past four decades we have established a government in exile and achieved almost full-fledged democracy. The Tibetan Diaspora has become a force to be reckoned with. Nevertheless, exile reminds us that our political status is ambiguous; that we float in a *bardo*[a] of statelessness.

Like all exiles, Tibetans too were driven to a state of homelessness by harsh circumstances. Yet, though physically deprived of home, Tibetans are not bereft within. Our strong traditional heritage and spiritual ethics guide us through the tangled web of political chaos, physical dislocation and existential uncertainty. Our struggle to re-root ourselves under thorny circumstances is a variegated canvas.

Exile Tibet binds three generations. Those who were born and grew up in independent Tibet and chased into exile after 1959; those who were born amidst the political upheavals of the communist Chinese takeover of the 1950s and sixties and came into exile at a tender age; and those who were born in exile. In that timespan we have witnessed a complete revision of our social structure. One of exile's positive changes was the increased access to education, and as a result of this a new wave of intellectual fervour flourished.

The rich Tibetan Buddhist philosophical heritage, which once remained within the confines of our monasteries, began to permeate the outside world. Tibet is now universally synonymous with concepts like Compassion and the Middle Path. However, this global awakening of interest in Buddhist studies has somewhat overshadowed our unique secular creative heritage in dance, opera, music, folklore and poetry, which remains barely explored.

Tibetan writing in English, which is a very recent flowering, is a small part of this secular culture. Though such works can be counted on our fingers, its future is undoubtedly bright. Led by the award-winning novel *The Mandala of Sherlock Holmes* by Jamyang Norbu, exile compatriots are in the mood for penning prose and verse (Tibetan: *snyan.ngag*), both in Tibetan and in English. Since the late seventies we have seen the publication of several poetry books in English by Tibetans.

Yet post-fifties exile Tibetans were not the first to express themselves in English. Prior to the mass exodus of Tibetans to India after 1959, a few highly privileged sons and daughters of Lhasa aristocrats, powerful chieftains and rich businessmen received modern educations in Christian boarding schools in Darjeeling and Kalimpong, and in the 1920s four boys were sent to an English public school by the Thirteenth Dalai Lama. But neither the aristocratic heirs, nor the schoolboys educated at Rugby, left behind any literary output worth mentioning. They largely disappeared into history, faceless and nameless.

Therefore, Gendun Choephel was probably the first-ever Tibetan to write poems in English. In 1927, when Tibet was enjoying her hard-won return to full independence, a young monk from Rebkong in the north-eastern province of Amdo arrived in Lhasa – full of vigour and bubbling with ideas. He was a rebel to the core. Desiring to broaden his knowledge, he later travelled to India where he roamed the streets of Calcutta and Varanasi and became what he called a "stray monk". Some biographers claim that he mastered the English language in six months.

Gendun Chophel was born in the wood-snake year of 1905. He was a brilliant student and became accomplished in Tibetan grammar and composition early in life. At 25 he joined Gomang College of Drepung Monastic University in Lhasa, where he created havoc in the debating courtyards with his antics and often unconventional, but brilliant, dialectical skills. However, without sitting for his Geshe Lharampa[b] examination, he left Drepung and headed south towards Sakya and eventually to India. During his fourteen years roaming India and Sri Lanka he lived like a vagabond. His sole craving was for knowledge. Knowledge, he hoped, that would one day benefit his beloved country – Tibet.

But when he finally returned to Lhasa, karma – *"that restless stallion"* – had turned against him. He was imprisoned for crimes of treason that were never proven, and underwent unimaginable suffering and humiliation. Out of jealousy, ignorance and narrow-mindedness, a few of Lhasa's ruling elite chose to destroy him. The land that he loved deserted him. Gendun Choephel passed away in 1951 at the age of 47.

Was he an exile compatriot? Politically he wasn't. But socially he was. He neither found his rightful place in the hierarchical monastic system, nor did his sharp, inquisitive mind and articulate mouth conform to the submissive and rigid social structure in yesterday's Tibet – especially in the eyes of Lhasa officials. Authority always seems to silence creative voices, since creativity means change and change means danger to those in power. Constricted by such a social climate, and in search of fresh knowledge, he left Tibet. During his self-imposed exile he missed his native land and longingly wrote:

> *"Rebkong, I left thee and my heart behind*
> *My boyhood dusty plays in far Tibet.*
> *Karma, that restless stallion made of wind,*
> *In tossing me: where will it land me yet?"* [1]

'I left thee and my heart behind' aptly foreshadows our plight today in exile. Perhaps, through his prismatic vision, he saw

that his fellow countrymen would one day wander in an alien land. In his own self-imposed exile Gendun Choephel experienced the same estrangement as we do today.

Due to severe economic limitations and lack of resources, very few Tibetans had the opportunity to fully master English in the early years of exile. It was around the late sixties and early seventies that a few began to write poetry in English. Chögyam Trungpa Rinpoche, one of the first Tibetan refugee poets, wrote profusely. Wandering foreign shores as a reincarnate spiritual master, he found innumerable subjects to write about, from the way women walk in tight skirts to mystic lines about the great lineage master Marpa.

Allen Ginsberg commented that Chögyam Trungpa's poetry represented the *"dramatic situation of someone who has realized the World as pure mind, and gone beyond attachment to ego to return to the world and work with universal ignorance, confront the spiritual-materialist daydream of Western World – and tell it in modernist poetry…"* This may be true, given the fact that Trungpa was a high-ranking Kagyud incarnation and a famous meditation master. As such, he may have written poems to transform the wayward moral lassitude of the western world he observed to a higher level. But the bulk of his poetry focuses more on muddier, mundane musings than on higher mystic matters. More than anything else, he was a Tibetan refugee in flesh and blood who had the intense desire to download his experience of an alien culture.

Trungpa himself talks of his poetry as evidence of how a Tibetan mind can tune into the western mind. This poignantly points out the inherent human instinct for survival and adaptation when faced with a sudden change in circumstances. Living in the west, Trungpa fine-tuned his intellect to western thinking, while remaining intrinsically Tibetan.

K. Dhondup, Lhasang Tsering and Gyalpo Tsering are writers of the Trungpa generation. The life of K. Dhondup is particularly poignant, given his early death and nationalistic fervour. He was born in 1952 in Tibet and died in 1995. In his short, but fruitful life, he wrote out of love for writing as much as *"out of a sense of duty to his country, culture and to the struggle of the Tibetan people for a free Tibet."* He was a historian, journalist and poet. With friends he launched *Lotus Fields: a literary magazine of Tibetans,* and *Dasar,* a Tibetan magazine, both of which unfortunately ceased publication after a couple of issues.

Today there are hundreds of budding young poets battling with scattered words and trying to chain them into a love poem or a desperate call for *Rangzen*. Seeds are sprouting. Soon the exile field will be a mass of flowers.

For thousands of young exile Tibetans born and growing up in squalid refugee camps, the imagined Tibet offers enchantment and a sense of belonging, thus reinforcing their pledge to the struggle for independence. There is an urgent longing and intense need to go back to their imagined Tibet.

> *"Let me sing a song*
> *The rhythm belongs to the mountains*
> *The words to the green pastures..."* (2)

So goes a poem titled *The Freedom Song* by Thupten N. Chakrishar, a young man born in India who has never seen Tibet. But his imagined Tibet is clear, crystallized in the high snowy mountains and green pastures of the Jhang Thang[d]. Such an idealized image is typical of the generation born in exile. Having never experienced their native land, their only recourse is to build a mental picture based on what they hear from the elders and see in photographs. It goes without saying that this imagined Tibet is far from the reality. Yet it offers them an opportunity to escape their otherwise dismal circumstances.

But being thwarted repeatedly in life by unfavourable situations, the exile youth have accumulated a deep sense of trepidation nearing a point of desperation. Some channel this energy into creative writing, as this book demonstrates. Many ventured into myriad avenues. A few are caught up in the ever-recurring dreams of drugs. The collective conscience expressed by them today has a root of deep resentment directed towards the U. N. and the exile government for their failure to find a workable political solution to the dilemma of Tibet's occupation.

> *"When I die, my friends*
> *Cut my head as my last wish*
> *And present it to U. N.*

> *So that they realize*
> *That the spirit never dies…"* (3)

The images that the exile poets create are the firsthand experiences of displacement and dreams.

> *"Our tiled roof dripped*
> *and the four walls threatened to fall apart,*
> *but we were to go home soon…"* (4)

So writes Tenzin Tsundue, a young writer-activist, in his poem *Exile House*. In this poignant description of a tile-roofed, leaky settlement refugee shack, there is the lingering hope "to go home" thus clearly highlighting the transitory state of exile. Here now, gone tomorrow and living as if everything was a series of momentary images.

In another poem he torments and bombards himself with questions of identity crisis.

> *"I am Tibetan.*
> *But I am not from Tibet.*
> *Never been there.*
> *Yet I dream*
> *of dying there.'* (5)

He doesn't find a suitable answer.

"Ask me where I am from and I won't have an answer. I feel that I never really belong anywhere. I was born in Manali but my parents live in Karnataka. I like to speak in Tibetan but prefer writing in English. I like to sing in Hindi but my tune and accent are all wrong. I have nowhere to call home…" (6)

This sense of estrangement is common to refugees across the globe, meandering into the space of others with initial hope and eventual disappointment. Only aspirations differ.

> *"I sing for myself the traveller*
> *The ever wandering vagabond,*
> *Eluded by promises and hopes,*
> *I sing...for the snow-sunk upland*
> *Where I want to die..."* [7]

A nostalgic and desperate ageing Tibetan whines in *Song of an Old Tibetan*. I often come across aged, withered Tibetans, tortured by years of surviving in exile. In death's mirror they see the past calling them back home, if only to die. It is a frantic call to a dying generation. Exile is a process, a state of constant movements and the last journey has to be homeward bound.

> *"Pick the white pebbles*
> *and the funny strange leaves.*
> *Mark the curves*
> *and cliffs around*
> *for you may need*
> *to come home again."* [8]

As the seasons change and years pass we dream of home. As the winds whisper upon the tantalizing Himalayan mountains, we long for freedom. And until inspired by happier themes to write about, we resolve to continue composing poetic notes from the footpath of exile existence...sometimes raging, sometimes musing.

Bhuchung D. Sonam
Dharamshala, 2004

Notes:

[a] the intermediated state between death and rebirth
[b] the highest monastic degree in Tibetan Buddhist philosophy
[c] freedom or independence.
[d] north-east Tibetan plateau where nomads roam; a huge, high landmass with rich pasture and a dry, cold climate.

1 *Rebkong,* Gendun Choephel, 'English Poems of Gendun Choephel' LUNGTA (winter 1995; pp. 12-13.)
2 *The Freedom Song,* Thupten N. Chakrishar, **YOUNG TIBET** published by the author; p. 8
3 *My Last Wish,* Thupten N. Chakrishar, **YOUNG TIBET;** p. 18
4 *Exile House,* Tenzin Tsundue, **KORA: stories and poems;** Published by Choney Wangmo 2002; p. 22
5 *My Tibetanness,* Tenzin Tsundue, **KORA: stories and poems;** p. 15
6 *My Kind of Exile,* Tenzin Tsundue, first published in OUTLOOK magazine
7 *Song of an Old Tibetan,* Bhuchung D. Sonam, **Dandelions of Tibet** published by Winsome Books India 2002, p. 50
8 *Horizon,* Tenzin Tsundue, **KORA: stories and poems;** p. 11

POEMS

Milarepa's Reply
Gendun Choephel

The earth and sky held counsel one night,
And called their messengers from northern height.
And came they, the storm fiends, the bleak and the cold,
They, who the stormwinds in grim fingers hold.

They swept o'er the earth, and then they called forth
That glist'ning maid from the far Polar North
In white trailing robe, the Queen of the Snow
And she sent her flutt'ring plumed children below.

And downward they flew in white, whirling showers,
While in black masses hung threat'ning the sky.
Some were large cruel sharp-stinging flowers
Some pierced his chest with a fierce-cutting eye.

Thus stormfiends, snow and icy frost blending
Came cold and sharply upon him descending.
On his half nude form these shapes did alight.
And tried with his single thin garments to tight.

But Milarepa, the Snow-mountain's child
Feared not their onslaughts, so cruel and wild.
Though they attacked him most fiercely and grim,
He only smiled – they had no power over him.

Oh Where?
Gendun Choephel

A city there is which lone does stand
In ruins mid bamboo trees
Hot blows the burning desert sand
Where dry shrubs sigh on thirsting land,
Where monkeys cry, and with these
Joins the shrill cry of the jungle cock
Where a maiden drives her scattered flock
To the tunes of the ancient lay.
Where an ox cart moves on its lazy way
And then halts for shade b'neath a jutting rock;
Oh, City, where is the day,
When on thy golden Throne sat Kings
Who held the Sceptre high in this place?

Hark, heareth thou Time's fleet wings?

Rebkong
Gendun Choephel

My feet are wandering neath the alien star,
My native land, – the road is far and long.
Yet the same light of Venus and Mars
Falls on the small green valley of Rebkong.

Rebkong, – I left thee and my heart behind,
My boyhood's dusty plays, – in far Tibet.
Karma, that restless stallion made of wind,
In tossing me; where will it land me yet?

Like autumn cloud I float, soon, there, soon here,
I know not what the fleeting moons may bring.
Here in this land of roses, fair Kashmir,
My years are closing around me like a ring.

Fate sternly sits at Destiny's hard loom
And irrevoked her tangled pattern weaves
The winds are blowing around my father's tomb
And I but dream of those still summer eves,
When – child – I listened to my mother's voice,
Whose stories made my youthful heart rejoice.

So far, so far I may not see those graves.
Ah, friend, these separation pangs are sore.
My heart is thrown upon the ocean waves
Where shall I at last reach a peaceful shore?

I've drunk of holy Ganga's glistening wave,
I've sat beneath the sacred Bodhi tree,
Whose leaves the wanderer's weary spirit lave.
Thou sacred land of Ind, I honour thee,
But, oh, that valley of Rebkong,
The sylvan brook which flows that vale along.

Manasarovar
Gendun Choephel

In the times now long forgotten
In the night of other ages,
When things were not as they now are
Lay the earth a lifeless body,
Cold and hard and all unyielding,
Like a maid in dreamless slumber,
Untouched by life's budding springmood,
Ere the glow of sunrise calls her.
And the sky looked down and saw her.
Gently then in stealth descending,
In the rose of early twilight
Stooped and kissed her in her slumber.
And behold her young heart heaving,
Throbbed her pulse, her eyelids opened
And those eyes, all filled with wonder
Shed the hot tears of her being.
Thus was born this Lake Himalayan,
Mother of the holy Ganga.

II

Mountain-wave, mystic and dreamy,
By thy shore does stand a maiden
And the rhythm of thy water
Stands she motionless and gazing,
Knows not where her flocks are straying.

The young hunter aims his arrow,
And, behold, he sees thy water,
And no more sees he the roebuck
Slacks the bowstring, flees the quarry.

When the sun in golden glory
Sheds his aureole o'er thy surface –
Standst thou like the shrine *Chamcapa*
But the white dreamrays of moon-light
Veil thee in a garb of silver,
In the robe of Milarepa.

A Letter to Marpa
Chögyam Trungpa

Solid Marpa
Our father,
The message of the lineage:
You are the breadwinner.
Without your farm we would starve to death.
Fertilizing
Plowing
Sowing
Irrigating
Weeding
Harvesting;
Without your farm we are poverty-stricken.
Your stout body,
Sunburnt face;
Ordering Dakmema to serve beer for a break;
Evidence of the three journeys you made to India
in you –
We sympathize with you for your son's death:
It was not the fault of the horse,
It was the seduction of the stirrup in which his foot was caught
As his head smashed into the boulders of conceptualization.
Yet you produced more sons:
Eagle-like Milarepa who dwells in the rocks,
Snow-lion-like Gampopa whose lair is in the Gampo hills,

Elephant-like Karmapas who majestically care for their young.
Tiger-like Chögyam roaming in foreign jungles.
As your lineage says, "The grandchildren are more accomplished than the parents."
Your garuda egg hatches
As the contagious energy of Mahamudra conquers the world.
We are the descendants of lions and garudas.

Haiku
Chögyam Trungpa

The beginner in meditation
Resembles a hunting dog
Having a bad dream.

His parents are having tea
With his new girlfriend –
Like a general inspecting the troops.

Skiing in the red and blue outfit,
Drinking cold beer with a lovely smile –
I wonder if I'm one of them?

Coming home from work,
Still he hears the phone
Ringing in the office.

Gentle day's flower –
The hummingbird competes
With the stillness of the air.

Burdensome
Chögyam Trungpa

The best minds of my generation are idiots,
They have such idiot compassion.
The world of charity is turned into chicken-food,
The castles of diamond bought and sold for tourism –
Only, if only they …
Oh, forget it.
What is the use of synchronizing?
Raccoons are pure animals, they wash their food.
Beavers are clever animals, they build their dams.
Hot cross bun is for Easter.
Men who care for themselves turn into heroes
Walking on cloud – but are not dreamers –
But performing a miracle.
Distant flute makes you happy and sad –
Only for the shepherds.
Long lines of generations are hard workers.
Glory be to the blade of grass
That carries heavy frost
Turning into dew drop.

Tibetan Pilgrim
Chögyam Trungpa

On the right, a mountain with juniper trees – at its foot a
　farmhouse topped with white prayer flags – is like a
　minister on a tigerskin seat.
On the left, a mountain covered with tamarisk trees – at its
　foot a farm filled with beautiful green wheat and barley
　– is like a queen on a silken throne.
Straight ahead, a rocky mountain rises above a monastery
　with glittering gold roofs like a king on a throne of gold.
An old pilgrim feasts his eyes on the richness of some
　merchant's camp, and patiently continues towards Lhasa.

Season's Greetings
Chögyam Trungpa

Emerging to the surface,
Such virginity
Blossoming as a teenager —
Wish I was Spring's father.

As the thunder gathers rain,
Flowers drink water;
Arrogant greenery has no hesitation.
Summer provides festivity, and life is worth living.

Hot pregnant mother
Preparing the eggs and sperm for the next year:
So voluptuous and ostentatious.
O Autumn, I will never go to bed with you,
But you come to dinner with me.

Constriction and rigidity of your martial law do not frighten me,
You give me chills and shivers;
But the way you decorate the mountains—
I admire your extravaganza.

As Skylarks Hunt for Their Prey
Chögyam Trungpa

As skylarks hunt for their prey,
I am captured by their stillness.

I experience neither thirst nor hunger,
But skylarks captivate my memory.

Whistling arrows on the battlefield remind me of my
general's bravery;
Should I run away or should I stay?

Buddhism neither tells me the false nor the true:
It allows me to discover myself.

Shakyamuni was so silent:
Should I complain against him?

PAN-DHARMADOLLAR
Chögyam Trungpa

Looking for cheaper restaurants,
Paying for expensive ties,
Are dualistic as much as Mohammed and the mountain.
Would the mountain come to Mohammed
Or Mohammed go to the mountain?
Sadat and Begin made a pact,
But who is going to achieve peace?
Vision and dollar are in conflict:
When there are lots of dollars,
There is no vision;
When there are no dollars,
There is lots of vision.
Clearly stranded,
Goodly rich,
Goodly poor,
Can't afford to pay for one's own tuxedo,
Can pay for one's luxury in the realm of buddhadharma,
Elegant waltz participation,
Contradiction after contradiction.
Why is a parrot green,
Speaking human language?
Why is a monkey ambidextrous,
Mocking humans?
Why do Americans mock the vajra kingdom?
They don't mean to,
They are merely being casual because they have no money,

Or they have too much money;
Therefore, they can come up with cheap proposals.
Will this go down in our history?
No.
The Noh play says:
Worshipping every deity is trusting in ancestral heritage.

For the cosmopolitan communication of dharma,
Let us have lots of ratna.
For the hermit who is in the cave in order to perpetuate
the practice,
Let us have lots of ratna.
For scholars who are translating buddhadharma into
Americanism,
Let us have lots of ratna.
For householder yogis who could practice tantra with
indestructible conviction,
Let us have lots of ratna.
For the freelancers who might give up their ego trips,
To accommodate and lure them into the dharma world,
Let us have lots of ratna.
For the young maidens who fall in love with the dharmic
man,
To create a truly genuine dharmic world,
Let us have lots of ratna.
For the warriors who fight for the sake of Shambhala
kingdom,
Who never leave their prajna swords behind,
Let us have lots of ratna.

For the administrator who never breathes for his own sake,
But is purely concerned about the facts and figures and morality of our organization of the vajra mandala,
Let us have lots of ratna.
For the vajra master who couldn't exist without the vajra world,
dedicating his life and yet receiving longevity nectar from others,
Let us have lots of ratna.
Money peeps,
Money tweaks,
However, money has never roared.
Lion's roar could be money.
Pay!
Due!
Accelerate!
Save!
Complain!
Bargain!
Let us save money by spending,
Let us spend by saving:
Sane money is free from dualistic territory.
For the Great Eastern Sun, frigid money is no good.
Computerized this and that is a kid playing cowboys and Indians:
Let us relax and be taut in our money world.
May there be Sukhavati of dollars.
May there be Shambhala kingdom with lots of wealth —
But wealth comes from waltz,

Waltz comes from dignity,
Dignity comes from consideration,
Consideration comes from being sane.
Let us spend,
Let us save:
The Great Eastern Sun saves and radiates.
Good for you –
Jolly good show to everyone –
Let us be genuine.

Highlands of Tibet
Chögyam Trungpa

Sheep roam on the meadows
    ornamented with blue flowers
The crow caws on the pine branch
    conversing with the magpie
Flags flutter on a cairn
    on a red rock peak where the vultures nest.
From the black tent amidst dark old yak folds
    smoke rises gently
    and the echo of the conches and drums of
    invited lamas is heard.
Irrepressibly happy and sad to see the
    highlands of Tibet.

Fresh Winds
K. Dhondup

Do not
    conjure up before us
        gruesome images of reality
            which cripple our hope
                shatter our dreams.
But leave us
    our dreams of the future
        yet to come and our
        visions of hope and realization.
Do not tell us
    'you are rootless,
        far removed from the sacred
            glory of your heritage...'
Leave us alone!
    Give us the chance to pursue
        our search for our
            shores and shapes.
Do not tell us
    'your philosophy is thin
        songs stale
            and beliefs tainted'
But let fresh winds
    blow over the snowy mountains
        shaking the slumbering cubs
            to rise and shine.

Exile
K. Dhondup

Exile
    is a marigold
        blushing luxuriantly
            in the morning sun
                luring turquoise bees
                from the beehives
                to suck their honey
Exile
    is a melody
        for the forgetful souls
            in search of wider horizons
                to cherish and conquer
A gold ring clasping
    round the white finger, exile
        is a memory of a beloved
            bleeding somewhere behind the
                high mountains

Lines to a Prostitute
K. Dhondup

I love you no less than my own self
This spring night I invite you to be my guest
You are my comrade; we are the leaves
the same juniper tree.

A thousand times
you have been plucked and mutilated
At the smouldering altar of human passion
But still you smile like the floating lotus
Gratifying the hungry gaze of a starved generation.

This spring night let us not waste
In prowling the horizons of physical passion
Nor delight in the twilight of sensual pleasure
But let us this night reveal to each other
Our scathed souls and heal the pangs
With courageous words of love and trust

To us the human streets have been cruel
Us they purged with their own sins
And on us they let loose their hungry dogs
Yet when the moon rises on a restless night
Our songs they seek; our streets they roam.
And like the juniper leaves
they set us afire
To appease their wrathful gods
of passion and ignorance.

A Poet's Poetry
K. Dhondup

Poets everywhere are the same
> The same songs come to them

A native drums
> in distant Africa
>> Perhaps his is the best poetry

From beyond those high mountains
> The robed lamas chant hymns
>> The most spiritual poems come to them

In New York
> where sky is lost to the sky-scrapers
>> She is turning her longing for nature
>>> The finest songs come from her

A child is born
> It screams
>> The screaming is poetry
>>> of the beginning of life

A tear is a poem
> A smile its celebration

While words are printed
> The best poems are written not on papers
>> But by the swans on the shores
>>> the winds on the highway

Cold Mountain Songs
K. Dhondup

For ages
I have been gone
from the home in the Cold Mountains

For ages
I have tried to sprout seeds
and keep singing the Cold Mountain songs

When round the evening fire
the old songs grow
I realize that I am not alone
In this search for home in the Cold Mountains

When the white cranes
take to their wings
I remember that I have lost
Even the way to home in the Cold Mountains

In my journey
from here to eternity
I often sing the Cold Mountain songs
I often watch the white cranes fly
Wishing they would lend me wings
For my homesick soul

Of Exile and Refuge
K. Dhondup

The lonely heart is a ship
    sailing in the starless
        stormy night

Groping without guidance in
    the gushing wind
        floating to and fro
            knocking its head
                breaking its soul
                    into a thousand
                    crying pieces.

Who knows what symphony
    the maestro has
        in store for the solitary
            ship sailing in the stormy
                sea of life?

Who knows what sunshine
    the spring has in its fold for the
        soul yearning for its shore
            and share of the spring songs?

Who when asleep would dream of
    the warmth of his beloved but
        he who has lost his when awake?

What the crowd
and the rush
    the screams and the songs,
        the gazing eyes and
            the frozen smiles
                mean escapes him.

Returning to his room
    in the starless night
        he has a thousand living
            memories breeding with the
                sad sound of exile and refuge...

After Spring
K. Dhondup

Confusion
    drifting in the sea
        floating like a leaf
            fallen from a tree

Spent and sad after spring
    walking the darkness
        drenching in the night rain

Crying for love
    panting for warmth
        dreaming of waterfalls, eating dry bread
            sleeping anxious nights
                in a stranger's bedroom

Awakening
    Realizing that now is the time to
        Retire and
            Rest in
                Retreat and
                    Reminiscence

Existence Anonymous
K. Dhondup

We are all late, except him
We are late for the ceremony of death,
Circumambulating
Meditating
Reciting
      the dead have been led to their
      kingdom of peace.

We have nothing
      save the joy of joining
      the ceremony of birth,
      the melancholia of dragging our days
      through the scathing stretch of
      our existence,
      our kingdom of life – birth and bread.

His was the existence of peace
Read magazine stories
Ate at restaurants
Slept on the asphalt road
Till he joined the ceremony of death
on a silent night.

With hardly a soul mourning
A prayer-wheel turning
for his rebirth...

Poisons of the Mind
K. Dhondup

A Tibetan *geshe*[1] came
in the morning
and spoke about poisons
that grow in our mind –

Poisons on which we depend
and have to depend
for our pleasures
and sorrows.

"Like flowers in a garden,"
he said.
"passion, hatred and anger grow."

"As the bees spend their lives
around the flowers
singing and sucking,"
he continued,
"Human beings spend their lives
with these poisons,
laughing
or weeping."

---

[1] A Tibetan Buddhist degree in philosophy, equivalent to a PhD. There are four levels of *geshe* degree; Lharampa, Tshogrampa, Dorampa and Lingsepa.

A Poem of Separation
K. Dhondup

Read half a poem of Walt Whitman
When I caught myself escaping
to my native shore
while you were still asleep

Through the mist of the early dawn
I heard your whisper
that you are not a song
but a poem of separation

And when in the evening you return
I see an injured poem
Bleeding like the dying soldiers
On the faraway hills of the Northern land

In the distant days when you were only a child
You used to dream of being a man of war
Now after losing all the battles you have fought
You still long to be a better soldier

And after years of escape and separation
You still recollect those native hills
Those prayer-flags, the echo of
the conches and highland dogs
Disturbing the still night
of the nomad valley

For long you have wandered over alien seas
Singing alien songs; stoned in discotheques.
But in your eyes I see the longing
for the Cold Mountain songs and
The long march back to our long lost home

You are a bridge to the future
for the poets and patriots:
You sing songs of sacrifice
And you beat the drums of destiny

And who comes to you
Must search for inspiration
In the very few lines
Of an injured poem

Broken Tune
K. Dhondup

Gazing at twilight's splendour
 at this threshold of life,
  I remember the long ago battles
   fought and lost again and again.

I also remember
 how they took away everything
  and left only a handful of
   joyless songs on our trembling lips.

Seeds scattered on sands thirst to bloom
 songs lost in chorus long to be heard
  But the stranger brought us the realization
   of the futility of sprouting on an alien soil
    of the anguish of clinging to the summer rainbows
     in a land full of hungry stones:
      a river that has run dry.

Yet songs of shackle and struggle
 shall surely survive,
  When the dawn breaks over the grey winter
   The sun will return to
    totter their tower of power.

Somewhere ages hence
 there will be a marching million
  To take up the broken tune
   ...of the long ago battles.

Mountains
Ngodup Paljor

Denali – the mountain endowed
With beauty and charms
The Queen of the mountains
In North America
When I see your bright face
I remember the smiling face
Of your sister Jhomo Langma[1]...
The Queen of the Earth
I grew on her lap
And I played with her children

[1] Tibetan for Mount Everest

untitled
Ngodup Paljor

I
Homer – the land gifted
With boundless natural beauty
Above the mountains brightly smiled
Below the cosmic dances of fish
In the middle gleeful songs of birds
The land of tall trees
And healthy people
Truly nature is generous
With nothing amiss – I write
With the trees for brushes
The ocean my ink
And the earth my paper

II
Wandering in the woods
Inhaling the tranquillity
Of nature
My heart was stolen by an old fat tree
There was something that
Pulled me to him
Perhaps his nobility
And endurance
To remain tranquil
Despite his isolation
From his friends

Ways of the World
Ngodup Paljor

I
When my bamboo flute's
Sound was deep
Birds of all feathers flocked around me
Without an invitation
Now this broken flute's shallow sound
Does not even draw the attention
Of seagulls

II
When my father left his body
I inherited a wooden cup
Some day when I die
Do you know what I am going
to leave for my inheritance?
A cotton stuffed zafu.

Dharmakaya
Ngodup Paljor

Morning
The blue Dharmakaya
Noon
The cloudy Dharmakaya
Evening
The windy Dharmakaya
Though I don't really know
What Dharmakaya is
Kharmakaya walks me

<u>Footnote</u>: In Mahayana Buddhism, Dharmakaya is the ultimate nature of the fully enlightened mind, a union of pure appearance and emptiness.

I Am What I Am
Ngodup Paljor

The wish of my Amala[1]
Was for me to become
A Buddhist monk
Dedicating my life to follow
The footsteps of the Buddha
But her wish was disappointed.
The wish of my father
Was for me to succeed as
A man of high degree
Earning my life working
For the government of Tibet
Yet...his wish too was unfulfilled.
Now, neither a monk
Nor a man of high degree
I have no specific wish to pursue
Nor am I living to have a wish
Generally, I follow the way of the clouds
I eat when I am hungry
And drink when I am thirsty.

[1] Tibetan for mother

Alaskans
Ngodup Paljor

Yes, Alaskans, we've driven enough plastic vehicles,
Yet they failed to take us to the Virgin Mother Land.
Now, let us Alaskans, drive our original vehicles,
A team of four legged.
Yes, Alaskans, we've eaten enough junk;
Yet it failed to satisfy our hunger,
Now, let us Alaskans, eat early sour-dough Bread.
Yes, Alaskans, we've drunk enough toxic water
Yet, they failed to quench our thirst,
Now, let us Alaskans drink the nectar of
The mountain stream,
Yes, Alaskans, we've danced enough topless
And bottomless
Yet, they failed to shape our bodies.
Now, let us Alaskans perform the dances of
Shamans and Northern Lights.
Yes, Alaskans, we've dug enough wells
That turned into Green Papers
Yet, they failed to fulfil our desires
And dreams;
Now, let us Alaskans, dig the deep
Wells of our minds and discover
Our own true nature.
Yes, Alaskans, if you are still confused
And lost in the stream of transformation,
Then, just be attentive audiences
And watch the show of the Cosmos.

Everything is clear, naked and quiescent.
There is beauty in the beginning,
There is beauty in the middle,
And there is beauty in the end,
This is the land where we live.

One with Nature
Ngodup Paljor

I

Since I lost the hiking trail
I sat under a virgin spruce tree
Leaning back against her feet
My mind drifted away...
With fleeting clouds

II

Now the wish of a poor poet
Is fulfilled
To retreat in the thick
Dense snow
And write simple poems

The Monk and the Nun
Lhasang Tsering

Their faces look the same —
But that is only natural
They are both Tibetan.

Their robes also look the same —
But that too is to be expected
Their Dharma is the same.

And it is not just their robes,
Nor also just their faces
Their vows are the same.

Why then is one of them —
The ample-bellied big one
Dashing around in a Toyota?

And why is the other one —
The frail, sad looking little one
Selling postcards by the roadside?

Well, that is simply because
The big one is a monk
And the other only a nun.

And while it is not true —
That all monks are rich,
Nor all nuns poor,

Yet, between the monk and the nun —
There seems to be a discrepancy,
Which does not favour the nun.

Footnote: This was written after Dr. K. Delbray from Scotland described to me an actual incident that took place near the main Buddhist stupa in McLeod Ganj. Dr. Delbray had stopped to ask a nun selling some postcards by the roadside why she was doing so. The nun was telling him that it was to raise funds to feed the other nuns in her nunnery when a new Toyota jeep, driven by a monk, noisily dashed by — raising a cloud of dust and a few questions.

Recollections
Tsoltim N. Shakabpa

my thoughts
lie in the green of the grass
nursing the tortured earth
remembering the past

my soul
sings the songs of the stream
feeding the river of life
recalling a dream

my body
dances on the flame of a fire
casting a net of light
awakening a desire

my reality
sleeps in the softness of snow
buried beneath a frozen dream
not wanting to know

Zero
Tsoltim N. Shakabpa

Zero!
such an ubiquitous number
it can mean nothing
or it can mean the world
it is the apotheosis of all numbers
it can mean financial disaster
or a financial windfall
it can bring a rude awakening
or a joyous moment of celebration
it can mean the end of time
or the beginning of a new life
with zero tolerance for nonsense
it can zero in to issue dense
it can be empty as zilch
or as pregnant as an egg
you can draw a sad or happy face from it
or leave it blank for the imagination
with zero you cannot be hero
infinitesimal is the power of zero

The Dalai Lama
Tsoltim N. Shakabpa

born a village child
raised a god king
he is a simple monk
burdened
with the plight of his people
who are oppressed
suppressed and transgressed
he is an ocean of wisdom
compassionate and forgiving
offering a carrot rather than a stick
hoping the red hawk
will release Tibet from its mouth
but the red hawk
does not a carrot want
it wants meat
but meat he has none
he is a vegetarian
He is the Dalai Lama

Torn Between Two Countries
Tsoltim N. Shakabpa

torn between two countries
separated by boundaries
one gave me birth
the other hearth
one gave me my heritage
the other my children's parentage
one taught me theocracy
the other gave me democracy
shattered dreams in one
in the other a life in the sun
for whom shall I my loyalty reserve?
which country shall I loyally serve?
torn between two countries
separated by boundaries
my heart will die in America
my soul will live on in Tibet

Made in China
Tsoltim N. Shakabpa

made in china
by unpaid prisoners
made in china
by starving prisoners
made in china
by brainwashed prisoners
made in china
by tortured prisoners
made in china
by dying prisoners
made in china
from dead prisoners
would you buy anything
made in china?

My Tibet
Tsoltim N. Shakabpa

my Tibet
sparkling in the snow
like diamonds in the sky
your mountain ranges endless
your air so pure

my Tibet
monks chanting prayers
nomads herding sheep
all so happy
all so fulfilled

my Tibet
the Potala
reaching to the heavens
the Norbulingka
a garden of Eden

my Tibet
the Dalai Lama
illuminating the country with wisdom
the people
enjoying ultimate peace and harmony

i long for yesteryear
i long for the future
i long for my Tibet

OM MANI PADME HUM[1]
Tsoltim N. Shakabpa

om mani padme hum
Tibet is my true home
no matter what the Chinese say
they cannot take that fact away
my land is a part of my heart
China cannot tear it apart
my people are a part of my soul
we stand united behind one goal
my culture is part of me
unique it is you can see
we pray and non-violently fight
with all our soul, body and might
we will get our country back
our land, people and our yak
Tibet is my true home
om mani padme hum

[1] the mantra of Chenrezig – Bodhisattva of Compassion

Haiku
Tsoltim N. Shakabpa

charity, the password for heavenly salvation,
has become the keyword for income tax evasion

dance, moon, dance – while the darkness is here
for tomorrow I shall devour thee with my light

my days are long and drawn
my ways are old-time song

mi casa su casa
my home is in Lhasa

like a dart in my heart
you keep tearin' it apart

imbedded in time
my pain doth chime

betwixt the first "hi"
and the last "goodbye"
life holds many a "sigh"

the thrill of victory
the agony of the feet

Calendar on the Wall
Tsoltim N. Shakabpa

my life
crouches on a yellow wall
months
buried beneath the unfinished month
last month
old Liberty Bell did chime
but last month
I had a country for the last time
this month
the sands of Egypt blows against Phaero's head
next month
the winds of change may present me an eternal bed
then I'll be free
from a life that crouches on a yellow wall

Nirvana
Tsoltim N. Shakabpa

life's music
is death to the living
death's drink
gives life to all the dead
in this pattern
fate knits our lives
inflames our ambitions
tortures our missions

tortured life!
break your friendship bond with fate
die eternally
living only in death
waking, sleeping
to the tune of the darkness
never gambling
in the light of life

In Case You Forgot
Tsoltim N. Shakabpa

in case you forgot
I've still got a lot
my enemies are forgettable
my friends are not
my fortune is destroyable
my integrity is not
my country is conquerable
my spirit is not
my bones are breakable
my words are not
my brain is destructible
my mind is not
my heart if divisible
my loyalty is not
my intellect is deceivable
my heart is not
my body is perishable
my soul is not
my heritage is traceable
my rebirth is not
my life is extinguishable
I AM NOT

In Search of Gesar's Sword
Gyalpo Tsering

Another lonely night
Among moss and shrubs
With the sky as my blanket
And a rock for my pillow.
When will this ever end…?

When will I find the sword?

Gesar didn't tell them all;
But that sword exists
Hidden in the mountains
Waiting to be retrieved.
Some say it's for the chosen one
But who is more chosen than I…?

If it's only for the chosen one
Why hasn't he come – why wait;
When all around death lingers
Like scavengers waiting
for the final sigh,
The dropping head – infinity.

The moon is too ashamed
To rise and glow with
His borrowed light;
And I am certain
He knows I'm right,

Yet he sulks coyly.

The stars mock me
With their distance;
Their cold light
Scattering the warmth;
Blinking sadistically
And leering at me.

Come messengers show me
Where it is buried
I've been here too long
Neither will I last forever
It's time now – it is
The moment do not delay.

The stream gurgles rhythmically
Through its cold course,
Leaving everything behind;
Without hunger nor anxiety,
Neither can it feel
Insulated by the night.

Let sleep come now
And take me swiftly through
This night of trials
To another weary day
In search of Gesar's sword
Buried in these mountains.

First Snowfall
Gyalpo Tsering

The raven caws
from above;
Below him
the rooftops
are all white;
And the prayer flags
Sag sullenly.

On the Wing
Gyalpo Tsering

'...... to Lithang and back'[1]
That's what he said
And I'm glad he did come back;
Though I guess he underwent a change.

Sometimes I begin to wonder
Why he didn't scoff at them;
After all who were they
To say he wasn't what he was.

Why didn't they wish him well
On his short winged flight;
Why didn't they say goodbye;
I am sure he felt the pain.

Over the years I wonder,
How many folks remember him,
While they sing his songs
for their love or over their *chang*[2].

---

[1] a prophetic song by the Sixth Dalai Lama on his disappearance and rebirth. See *Songs of the Sixth Dalai Lama* translated by K. Dhondup, Library of Tibetan Works and Archives, Dharamshala
[2] traditional Tibetan barley beer

Cold Frost
Gyalpo Tsering

Yesterday
Like the sun
You shone
Your golden rays …
 on me.

Today
Like the night
You unfold
Your black wings;
While cold frost
chills my heart.

To You from Exile
Gyalpo Tsering

Hello! And greetings,
Is this just enough
Or are there more words
That you can accept
Without facing a public trail?
Can I send you love
Or more bread to eat?
Whichever way
I think it's the same.

Since no cranes are left
I can only send my
Message with the winds;
Hoping
That they don't deprive you
of that too.

I only knew you and mum
Since the age of four,
No names; no photographs;
Just you and her.
And me, I don't think
You remember, at all,
You don't let it bother you.
Your tears are precious fluids
They are dear to you;
They keep you going

from day to day
Not aimless but
with a passion.

I wish I could hear
Just one note of
Your mellow voice
Recorded on a tape;
Just a single note –
Even though the atom is split
And the moon is conquered
My wish remains
A far fetched fairy-tale.

Are you warm and are you happy?
No, I don't think so,
But all the same
Your answer must be 'YES'
Do they take you out
To a theatre or a show?
And can you pray
Very earnestly
Like you used to?
Even then the answer
Must be a 'YES'.

Although I dream
You are still alive
And sincerely believe it;
But at times

I begin to doubt.
Even if you are dead
I suppose your answer
Will be a 'YES'.

I can keep on writing more;
Even more than all the books
But of what use will they be,
Since you are no nearer
To me than the stars.
Yet I have hope that
No man can dim;
To see you and mum
Free at last.
To you I write from exile
To you my hope and faith
To you — —

At the End of the Rainbow
Gyalpo Tsering

I have no summer; no marigolds
No dandelions ride in the gentle wind,
   No dreams, no pot of gold at
    My end of the rainbow.

I have only winter and the cold;
The starless night sounds whine
   Icy fingers point back at
    The other end of the rainbow.

Heaven thaw this icy world
Share the summer and the marigolds;
Soothe the night; and the long wait
    At the end of the rainbow.

The Weatherman (Ngagpa-la)
Gyalpo Tsering

As the rain clouds gather in the sky
The wind goes howling by.
Trees sway and flowers nod
Their heads…and note
Their defeatest attitude.

While on a hillock sat Ngagpa-la,
Kangdung[1] raised and sprinkling flour
On the incense fire.
Mumbling charms…higher
Still the smoke clouds ride the wind.

In the streets and fields where children play,
Men and beast alike make hay.
Children lift their heads
In glee…but heed
The anger of those distant clouds.

Still undaunted Ngagpa-la prays on,
Clouds hear his *Kangdung* horn.
His strong incense dispels
The winds…then falls
The sun on the valley of Lhasa.

---

[1] a tantric horn made of human thigh bone

The Nomad I
Gyalpo Tsering

He sits and gazes, with a song upon his lips
While his yak herds graze: he and they
Are a part of that immense, grassy waste
That stretches desolately where wild winds rage.

All through the day he sings; all else about
Him was as if glued to his hoarse voice.
Strange melancholy sails on the sea of grass,
At times to be outsung by the wind's howling song.

At intervals he gathers up his *chuba*[1] sleeves
To crack his woven wool sling; at its sound
His shaggy friends throng onwards to fresh grass,
Coarse, but sweet enough fill until dusk.

Here there are no birds or the smell of men
For miles on end, only his grazing masses,
Like islands on a calm sea, smeared with coloured life,
To welcome a lone traveller, baffled by isolation.

Then, when day wanes and wild winds grow chill,
He gathers the herd with gleeful wolf calls
And shambles behind them, home to the distant tents,
That greet and balm the day's toil with rest.

---

[1] traditional Tibetan dress for men and women

The Nomad II
Gyalpo Tsering

As the stars fade in the morning sky
He drinks his butter tea,
Wrapped in his wool-lined quilt
While his wife gently milks the *dri*[1].

He recalls the sleepless night
And the damned wolf pack
That stampeded his yaks beyond
The stone fence that he had built.

Now the sun seeps through the tent flaps
And the tea kettle lies empty on the floor.
Soon the wind will rise and he before it
Must prepare the blue-print of a new day.

The urge to move on disturbs his thoughts
That runs the breath of the grasslands,
In search of freedom to another world
Where the prospect of new pastures await.

---

[1] female counterpart of yak

The Nomad III
Gyalpo Tsering

I slowly gather up my shaggy herd
And prepare them for the lowlands,
While wolves get hungrier and brave
The sun's rays that freeze with the breeze.

Already I feel the longing to remain free
Here where I can sing and train my thoughts
On matters that follow no boundaries,
But nature overrules my wondering too far.

Nine loads of butter wrapped in gut
Lies freezing while I thaw the saddle-bags,
For busy days in the cities of butter-lights
Too crowded; too sinister for the wide spaces.

My friends can bare the cold and the storms
That blankets my grassland thoughts,
Wind and yet clear of soggy-dung smoke
Trapped in the cold hearth where the fire burns.

The Hermit
Gyalpo Tsering

In the cave where silence reigns,
King of darkness;
The humble Hermit stays.
In the Hermit hunger strains,
The coming vision.

In the gloom where winter plays,
Shadowed dampness;
The humble Hermit prays.
In his soul and sallow face,
Serenity wades.

In his world where desire wastes,
Attachment fades;
The humble Hermit waits.
On his tattered robes dust flees,
The vision clears.

In the cage where his heart beats,
Faint hope sleeps;
The humble Hermit dreams.
In the cave silence reigns
King of darkness.

The Broken Plough
Norbu Zangpo

Now that our plough has broken
What shall we turn it into –
A pen:
A gun:
Or shall we just burn it
And forget there ever was one?

To Boat People
Norbu Zangpo

Oh, you brave, brave people
I greet you in exile!
You have like me become
An orphan of this world.

And like me, you will never ever
Know what lies ahead now:
But you must be patient
While we remain exiled.

Now that the worst is over
You must learn once again
To smile at the rising sun:
And to start all over again.

America
Norbu Zangpo

I bare my breast to you
Because you have ceased
to be Liberty's citizen:
You have cut down her sword
And used it for your end.

The Wish
Norbu Zangpo

There's no time to waste on you
You're just a wretched peasant
An ungrateful serf to loath:
Your impertinence deserves
Fifty lashes from my whip.

Take him away and lock him up
In the darkest cell and if he dares
Let him break out alone to freedom:
If that's what he wants he'll not love
Long enough to share it with anyone.

This piece of land he calls his own
Is mine to do with as I please
Sell it: loan it or give it away:
Even his worthless life is mine
To sell: Loan or do it away!

Ha! ha! ha! Freedom he says:
The poor wretch wants freedom—

Rainbow and a Glass Cage
Tenzing Sonam

And if day was to dawn
against this cumbersome burden
recycled in phases
each an entity
separate in distance so infinite
as to be linked

a misty evening sun
is feebly waltzing with
a strain of melancholic sax
that floats in thousand visions
a precise slant of moonbeam
fragile in its nuance
lights the road
up to the mountain
this cricket sings
the song of night

Yet have I laboured
in the catacombs of my mind
drowned and reborn
in the quicksand of time

These lakes these hills
these many forked paths
loud music gay dancers
perfumed smoke and wine

A stillness reigned
across the valley
and we downed this drink
to prolong the night

to the chant of life
we make our choice
to the song of the wild
I will leave you my senses.

Plea — (Dance of the Shadows)
Tenzing Sonam

there are all-consuming shadows
that dance in my mind
there is the bird of paradise
and there is the bird of apocalypse

o anais; patron-queen; giver of life;
I am floundering in a gulf
between two shores,
fiery imps and desert winds
have assailed my senses —
transported me to crossroads
of confusion

deliver me to the path of eloquence!

o father;
do you watch the skies
and hear the song of the spring bird
or do you see the cracks on your walls
and watch dust gather on your
window sill?

May Musings
Tenzing Sonam

sometimes you tell me
to throw out my arms
when I've caught glimpses
of perfect light
blue-gold butterflies
ringed by the glow
warm rocks and high hills
showing me the way

sometimes you
show me
the gates in the sky
a cool breeze hushes
the eternity of thoughts
a brown leaf drowns
in yesterday's puddle.
sometimes, o but sometimes
I touch
your perfect beauty
for a second

Vignettes in Random
Tenzing Sonam

there are things in my mind
they are formless
even beyond space
or time
there are things in my mind —
a gentle touch of colour
a certain odour
or a frozen frame
it is evanescent
like concrete wisps

(a thin shaft of sun ray
broke through my curtain
frenzied intricacy
of dust in dance)

my worlds are caged hues
of waterfall in wind
of moon beam on mountain
I paint on the canvas
of my mind's spread eye

so many withered flowers
and all this splendour
there is love yet
for the warrior of beauty.

untitled
Tenzing Sonam

A poetic dilemma, alas !
what strange proportion
of reality – unreal in
this surreal cube – waxed
in a transfigured blur.
Yes, action in suggestion,
force in hint, swaying in
an infinitesimal shudder
over the void blockade –
of a precipice that descends
into oblivion, surely,
since I feel it not, and yet
am compelled.

To complete in incompleteness,
To decide in question,
To answer in illogic,
To write in despair.

A desperation that justifies
a freeze in the flow
a snap in the wind.

Do words spin the rationale
that reason weaves in logic?
Strange patterns then.

Burlesque
Tenzing Sonam

Baba sells dreams at the steps of a *masjid*
among the squalor rises an archaic memory
if this stench of low-ebb humanity repulses you
know also that the song-birds play in the filth
and bring with them the perfume of the hills...
and there are dreams to be bought at *baba's masjid.*

Autumn Love Dance - time for reckoning
Tenzing Sonam

I am weary of this colourless wall
engulfing my senses
blinding my faculty
merging me into
its insipid self

Rejuvenate me!
I have grown old and
this torpor is deadly
my limbs are corrugated
with the vapours of disuse
my mind corrupted
by mundane pleasure

Aeolus rides the autumn wind
races through the rusting trees
brown leaves gather in his wake
dancing to the fading light

there is an old tune
that rings in the valley
a ballad of lament
of turning points
the path is strewn
the song will end
and the time has come
to fly down south

(these withered flowers provoke
my senses
there are continents yet
for the intrepid voyager)

Song for the Dead
Tenzing Sonam

The orange hue of filtered
sunlight, in the evening of
day, was reflected within
these forgotten stones.
          in the Spring
you have flowers and the
songs of birds......
Will you believe me, that
yours is the eternal song?
The leaf-song and the life-song;
the earth song.
          your earthly
remains achieve what through
life was failed,
or not realized......

Song for a Season
Tenzing Sonam

hide not your face
in the sorrow of
misty shroud,
I will send you a dream
on archless wings.

there are strung-prayer
flags, frayed and faded
in memory of a time
lost to the wind.

on this chilly morning
there is subdued despair
somewhere in the dark recesses,
a forgotten cry
in the labyrinth of my mind
song mingles with shadows.

a flute solitarily floats
by the old shepherd's slope
a tune for a moment,
but is swallowed
in the silhouette
of twilight birds
musing on an autumn branch.

here is my song

a song for a season,
from the carnival of yesterday
is resurrected a dream.

If I Die
G. C.

If I die my dear ones
Don't cry for me
For I never cried for anyone
It's time I part with me…
Your prayers will not hear me
For I have parted with my hearing
Your worries will not affect me
For I will still be looking for compassion…

So be kind and compassionate
While you can be compassionate
Once you go beyond the cold tombs
It's too cold
And begin my way to another womb…

Destination
G. C.

With Mama's loving care
Daddy's warm smile
With home's soothing air
I can go many miles
Towards their destination...
With society's pompous system
People's exploded expectation
School's stereotype education
I can step many miles
Towards their destination...
With Buddha's guidance
With Dharma's wisdom
With all my devotion
Opens heavenly kingdom
It's my humble destination...

I Wish To Be Buddha
G. C.

You are nothing but everything
So simple yet so complicated
So near yet so far away
Walking under the roof of the sky
Sleeping on the bed of earth
Walking on the truth
Surrounded by compassionate feeling
Your life is my guide
More than anybody's fantasy
You are so eternal so balanced
More than these words
My feelings are strong
How I wish I am Buddha

Reality and Illusion
G. C.

Reality and illusion
They are too big for me
They always come in motion
To pinpoint is too hard for me
Past was once a future
But it's all broken promises and wills
It was once beyond time and today's future
Still filled with promises and will
Knowing that these will soon break
Its not concept or mind though
Like my own form…it will soon break

Pass By
G. C.

I have seen many pictures
I heard so many lectures
But pictures never seem to end
And lectures only confuse me in the end
Just hold for a moment
And say Hello! To yourself
It's the best picture ever
The most comforting lecture
I love and cherish the moment
And watch it pass by

Visions in Snippets
G. C.

Life delights and death mourns
But life goes on
Delight smiles and pain frowns
But emotion feels
....

I was born naked
But dressed by my mom
May be conscious is also naked
Dressed by thinking
....

Mountain looks in the sea
For his image and found
The sea is green
....
And little road
Yellow as my race
Dust of the dust
They must not bruise you

Let Us and Let Us Not
G. C.

Let us not do for the glory
Let us not do for the history
Let us do for the pain we are feeling
Let us do for the freedom we are dreaming
Let us not fight for regional right
Let us fight for Tibet's right
Let us not fight for any possession
Let us fight for Tibet's position
Let us not fight for any path
Let us fight anyone who destroys any path
Let us not fight for stereotype democracy
Let us build a genuine democracy
Where we can enjoy openness and intimacy.

untitled
G. C.

I am just a soul in a fix
Crying for the right direction
My mind is so mixed
It's in total confusion
Time is made of tenses
But moments are gone when it's gone
I am the judge of the senses
But I always have moments to feel
It's neither me nor life
Moments are still pure
Only neither can be conceived.
....
Do not listen to my words
look at my actions
I am a very worried man
I am a very desperate man
Please understand me
It will save me from going crazy.
....
I feel myself
standing in the wilderness
cold
alone
empty
beauty all around me
pain constricting my heart
the road of life lies long and empty

and no balm exists to sooth me
of this loss and broken heart.

A Matter Not of Order
Tsering Wangmo Dhompa

I

You eat with your right hand.
Prop the broom away
from your body. Strike.
A roof of wool, a bed of skin.
A follicle for food. A hand of error
and infliction is given to all.
The left hand heeds
prayer beads. The left hand
signals retreat.
What is your good name?
Where are you from?

II

I was taught not to ask for more.
I took the smallest pieces,
left the last on the plate to deities,
bullies and elders. Train eyes,
the elders said, to want
what is already yours. So I stayed
out in the woods till jackals howled
and picked from the streets what was
lost or cast off. Sang songs
to a kindergarten teacher
who wore pink checkered dresses

and spoke in English when cross.
Now bigger is a sign of competence.
Was my heart stitched for this?
I am drifting into a world of enquiry
to quantify, qualify, even as
around me, summer performs.
Beetles, coal stunned in sun.
And little birds in grey
sing madly for food or love.

III

You are placated
with offerings
hollow as midnight's ankles.
Day life postpones impulses
to the future as though it sits
ahead with a symbol for permanence.
In night life you dream
a daughter. Skin a beast.
You can tell you are good.

IV

I know you by your walk
because we are from the same country.
If you were here to give safe passage – mosquitoes,
daddy-long legs, molluscs underwater – would
be left to their job. West surrenders
to a new language. Bellwether.

Billingsgate. Bivouac. Let us go
south. Let us go east. We come to be
courted. Or hands emptied.

V

Conquered by ingredients: we replace salt
with sugar. Butter with milk.
We believe others know better
because we've arrived to find our place taken.
Your hands blunt from obeying.
Your name is happy days
and wisdom. What cannot be explained
is accepted. Our forefathers went
to bed with salted butter tea in their bones.
You are living the life given.
You drink sweetened tea at three
in the afternoon. Adjust cup to saucer.
Your gullet adhering to silence.

VI

Once in the year of the iron horse, the river
changed course and your house was built.
I am the foolish one seeking old treasures
when monkeys still steal from our verandas.
When we say rock, shell, sand, labour is not
intended. Rocks selected for you.
The lines in my palm follow weather predictions,
stock predictions, thinking experts must be heeded.

Must consistency be an illusion? Here, pick up
dandelions, watch seeds bellow into air.
Wish to desire. It's the human way.

VII

The appearance of a crow
throws the morning into distemper.
Children's haircuts are postponed.

New plans are made after referring
to numerical charts and the whereabouts
of the mad dog last seen chewing a shoe
at the gate. The elders remember events
related to a crow's previous entry. It's not
just the coming winter. Fire crackers go off
in the neighbourhood. Someone is preparing
her nuptial bed; a room of newly acquired
tokens. Dogs keep their normal routine.
Everything is partially revealed.

VIII

How simple it would be
and to our best interest
to offer what we have to bandits.
We have climbed the mountain
passes, offered prayers and ruminated
on the possibility of tumbling over
the edge. Many hours of rain and the road

is a river. Grasslands bronze as nomads
move closer to their winter holes.
This world is a lie. I think of all
the futures you will miss. Life goes
by the centre. We are drinking.
We are eating.

The water song
Tsering Wangmo Dhompa

M's mother was so beautiful her father hid her in a box. I choose to believe this version of a story even though reason compels me to question the existence of one such box. Wooden or steel. Details make it permanent.

Cement roofs do not entertain the reality of rain. Only when the curtain is drenched do you acknowledge it.

I am reminded of Jetsun, how after dipping her feet in the Ganges, thought she felt a little flutter in her head.

After my hands are washed, I undo my altar. The offered is erased from possession even as it remains.

After the dishes are put away, after the curtains are drawn, some woman will make love.

It is not the knowing but the moment after saying *ah* that pleases.

A ritual is a place of wisdom. In time you learn how much water exactly fills seven prayer bowls.

Somewhere must be a photo of M's mother. When I see it, I will understand why M never told me she jumped from a bridge and tried to take a Chinese soldier with her.

A lama said I was her reincarnation. I have the same underestimated will. M's will is a more flamboyant so it is suggested I learn from her.

Horses, a French man once said, see only one path. He was also referring to me.

After losing an image, you learn to live in sentences.

The new jug for the prayer bowl does not know its own ability to contain water.

Everything is isolated. And dependent.

Third lesson
Tsering Wangmo Dhompa

When the elder died in her sleep, Samten was dancing to Nepalese rap under looms suspended at an abandoned carpet factory.

No explanations were made by the Tibetan doctor. Impermanence, he said when asked for the fourth time.

The elders swarmed in greys and browns. Brought rituals to keep his mother's wandering soul in non-life. Too many illusions, they said, in *bardo*[1].

Food and sweet juniper incense were sent to the scattered mother out in the garden.

No more tears, the lama said. It is the dead who suffer, not the living. He said the departed one's senses were magnified. She wasn't aware of her own death. Think of her living in death. Think of her in her imagined body.

For forty-eight days, Samten lived with prayers and clung to her new birth.

Later he remembered how his body had refused to move at a certain moment on the dance floor. His head, he said, had not adhered to the beat he had practiced to. He was all out of step with his partner.

Now she is dead, the lama said. Do not speak her name out loud. She is now your mother who is no more.

Later he remembered how he loved seeing his mother who was no more with her shopping bag in the market. Always, meat and a bunch of coriander.

Always, a magenta umbrella folded in her hand.

Later he remembered the largest pieces of meat were given to him.

---

[1] the intermediate state between death and rebirth

Hibernation
Tsering Wangmo Dhompa

Grass was refusing growth in eastern Tibet. The rainmaster struck his *damaru*[1], lay his cheek against the river and called for rain.

M said life too was a matter of preparation and adjustment. We lit butter lamps at the stupa and watched a trickle of light gather on the Buddha's eyebrows. Butter smog as air.

The Tara statue had tears in her eyes. The caretaker produced the piece of scrap paper he had used to wipe it off. Words ran into each other where water touched ink like meandering veins in a frayed wrist. The monk blessed himself with it as I read:

100 kilos of sugar
100 packets of Taj Tea
Total = 2,000 rupees.

For days people stood in line to give offerings to the statue. Prayers fell as the spine of streets were wet for weeks. M kept us close to her, burned incense all day and said something was in the air. Water continued to thrash the gullies.

Mosquitoes chewed the night to pieces. Then sunlight.

The elders said the chief oracle of the Tibetan government in exile had predicted we were closer to negotiations but he could hear cries of women slicing the air before him. When he dropped to the floor, he had a hint of a smile. M said no place was safe and offered the first burst of marigolds to the deities.

Very little made sense. News came of a day's rain in the east.

After life. After life. So elders comb their prayers beads.

[1] a small two-faced ritual drum

Exile House
Tenzin Tsundue

Our tiled roof dripped
and the four walls threatened to fall apart
but we were to go home soon,

we grew papayas
in front of our house
chillies in our garden
and changmas[1] for our fences,
then pumpkins rolled down the cowshed thatch
calves trotted out of the manger,

grass on the roof,
beans sprouted and
climbed down the vines,
money plants crept in through the windows,
our house seems to have grown roots.

The fences have grown into a jungle
now how can I tell my children
where we came from?

---

[1] a tree usually planted as fencing; flexible and flourishing

Horizon
Tenzin Tsundue

From home you have reached
the Horizon here.
From here to another
here you go.

From there to the next
next to the next
horizon to horizon
every step is a horizon.

Count the steps
and keep the number.

Pick the white pebbles
and the funny strange leaves.
Mark the curves
and the cliffs around
for you may need
to come home again.

The Third Side of a Coin
Tenzin Tsundue

The head,
the Tail
and the Ring
are the three sides
of a single Coin.

It's extremely difficult
to sit on the Ring
(the Third Side)
of the single Coin.

It wouldn't stand
on its Ring.
If it did,
you couldn't sit on it.

If you managed
to do that too,
you couldn't see
at the same time
the both sides
of the single Coin.

While in a single gaze,
you'll fall,
soon and surely,
to one side

of the single Coin.

Good-Bad, True-False,
Patriot-Terrorist,
mostly form
the two sides
of the single Coin.

But the Third Side?
Nobody knows
and nobody wants to know.

As for me, I can't see
more than my sphere
within the horizon-ring.

Now don't tell me
to see through
to the other side.
Even in my own sphere
I am quite myopic.

I can't even make
a Coin stand on its ring
and you're asking me
to ride it!

The Flower and I
Tenzin Tsundue

She drew that tiny flower
a pretty little flower
with a scent and colour,
And I, the butterfly
like a tiny simple fly,
hovering over the flower.
But she painted mine
in her own design.
I gave it feelers
two crooked feelers.
And that was all
It was mine.

untitled
Tenzin Tsundue

The green, green field
from here to the horizon
is dotted,
by three small dots
almost in the centre,
a bit towards the left –
three plastic bags.
A blood red one,
a liver brown one
and a bone white one.
So when the wind blows
and the golden green waves
the plastic bags float
bloated.
But struck to the green, green field.

Spider-webbed
Tenzin Tsundue

The hostel mess is closed
and I got no money.

The vacation has just begun
and it's already lonely here,
with a few more cash-strappeds,
haunting the empty corridors
and the dozing old man.

Dried eyes, pale, as if sucked in
by the multitude of empty rooms,
goggling at each other in a ring
as if to say 'I am also here'.

I passed by one, stared at him
and he stared at my gullet.

Sometimes, someone lightly blows
a thin tune into the mouth organ,
only for it to vanish somewhere
into the tight hinges of the closed doors.

Before I swallowed my next glob
of saliva, I need some water.
My water-bottle on the table
is spider-webbed to the table lamp.
A mosquito caught, flits and freezes.

My clock reads six
Is it morning six o'clock?
Or evening six o'clock?
Where is that bloody sun!

Looking For My Onion
Tenzin Tsundue

I peel and peel and peel
      looking for my onion.
And when my eyes are full,
      hands stained,
scattered peelings stare at me,
I realise I actually had one.

I am a Terrorist
Tenzin Tsundue

I am a Terrorist.
I like to kill.

I have horns,
two fangs
and a dragonfly tail.

Chased away from my home,
hiding from fear,
saving my life,
doors slammed on my face,

justice constantly denied,
patience is tested
on television, battered
in front of the silent majority
pushed against the wall,
from that dead end
I have returned.

I am the humiliation
you gulped down
with flattened nose.

I am the shame
you buried in darkness.

I am a terrorist
shoot me down.

Cowardice and fear
I left behind
in the valley
among the meowly cats
and lapping dogs.

I am single,
I have nothing
to lose.

I am a bullet
I do not think

from the tin shell
I leap for that thrilling
two-second life
and die with the dead.

I am the life
you left behind.

Pyre of Patriotism
Topden Tsering

Somewhere in that capital of Aryabhumi
When the air sizzled like autumn leaves on fire
On a pavement strewn with dirt and defecation
Where beggars battled for space with mongrels
As if in prototype of India's chaotic fate
As if in reflection of a world gone awry
There fluttered unabashed and in incongruous glory
A flag with two snow lions and a radiant sun
Aloft a makeshift tent of blue polythene walls

Heavy hearts murmured prayers of redemption
Swollen eyes wept silent tears of grief
Ancient hands clasping rosaries bright
Hundred feet shuffled about in nervous pace
Stirring up in that stifling Delhi heat
A swirling dust of fractured foreboding

Around and about that battered tent
Wherein lived the hunger strikers six
Courageous souls now reduced to bones
Hollowed cheekbones and immovable spirits

Hope lived that day
That summer of 1998
When famished bodies defied human endurance
And half-shut eyes beamed conviction divine
When within that ragged yet emotion-charged shelter

Rangzen seemed within the reach of a lifetime

Then reality raised its monstrous head
Its tentacles stretched out in evil greed
And not before long in its deadly grip
Human faith shuddered one more time
Dead but not as yet outside heaven's gate
Condemned forever to that border to purgatory

Hope died that morning
That early morning of April 28
When desperation took to its naked dance
When freedom was sought on the altar of sacrifice
When a martyr was born in the exile Tibetan world

A blazing figure ravaged by flames
A human pyre of supreme patriotism
Half limping, half jumping
Half dying, half exulting
Straddling across the frantic stage of Now
His hands joined over his head in supplication
His cackling lips shouting one more time, one last time
"*Bhod Rangzen*" "Free Tibet"

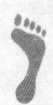

Guilty in Love
Topden Tsering

A kiss immortalized in Kodak frame
I hold dearly in my quivering hands
A cut into the flashback of time
When in her lived that love for me

Our lips frozen in solemn promise
Of emotions deeper than the oceans deep
When into her heart whispers I blew
Of the three-lettered word, my only wealth

To her muse, a nervous bard I played
In distant days not more than a decade half
When in her lived a love for me
For which I died a thousand deaths

Now alone and naked I stand in my room
Strewn around me, the shards of my broken dreams
The icy walls bellow judgement of shame
From every crack, I hear a faint echo of humiliation

And so my head hangs in muted ignominy
As guilty I stand in love's divine court
Within the icy walls of my crumbling room
Alone and naked, stripped even of that three-lettered
word, my only wealth

For Appearance and Worse
Topden Tsering

It is interesting this cacophony of words
Where each unto himself an oracle's mantle takes
Slashing left, right and centre
With the precision of a ninja sword
A conviction, either forced or found
In a goal, either *Rangzen* or nowhere land

Invisible fingers dancing away on keyboards
Their grip as yet to the contours of a trigger unknown
Hearts raging with a freelancing surge of passion
Churning soups of rhetoric, sprinkled with icy spice

But it is interesting this cacophony of words
Where names are called, histories re-visited
Dogmas criticized and radicalism at half-prices sold
Chests-thumping in gorilla ecstasy
Where free speech banana in the dozens devoured

And so the breast-beating continues
Some Laloo Prasad Yadav in the making
Others Hitler, his moustache shorn by half
Then there be Phoolan Devi, if not a Napoleon
Joan of Arc a few, only her armour lipstick-stained

In between them the Mandela or is it Guevara
The former a cautious, boxer-turned-pacifist
The latter a rebellious modern-day Quixote

Upright Nehru, or is it the chuckling Gandhi
Roosevelt, Geronimo or cigar-chewing Churchill
Gun-planting Bhagat Singh or bare-chested Azaad
Blued-eyed Lion of the Desert
Or Mao with his tobacco-stained teeth

Either all or one of them, better still none
My fuming friends in "Tommy Hilfiger" camouflage
Cigarette for a gun, chewing gum for bombs
Icons-in-the-making all of them
The gorillas soon to be guerillas

Conflict
Topden Tsering

In my dreams I see three MIGs
Flying over Beijing
Bombing to rubble
The entire Zhongnanhai compound

Three young Tibetans, fiery young Tibetans
Or two Tibetans and a supporter, a supporter enraged
Or One Tibetan and two supporters, driven to the brink
Or three supporters, fiery three supporters

At dawn, when beyond the New Mexico plains
The sun shimmers with its first rays
Into the blue, three fighter jets take off
Screaming *Rangzen*[1] into the void of Now

Over the walled city, just above the dreadful enclave
Where dwell the bureaucrats, their hands blood-stained
Fed on the lives, dreams and hopes of Tibetan people
Fat men in black suits, red flags, black hearts
Over the walled city
The jets hover for a fraction of a minute
Their wings the colour of silver bullets
While underneath them
Flashes past
Red velvet of fractured memories

..........1959

Tibetans dying in Chinese gulags....
......Killed on the streets
Dark dungeons of freedom nowhere to be seen…
..........Raped nuns
exile, homelessness, ghostliness
Tibetans...the dying breed

Tenzin, (or is it Jacob?)
Presses upon the red button
To the hum of his Om Mani Padme Hum
The bombs drop, in silent whispers

Jiang, Zhu, Zhou, Mao
All of them, with their degrees in Engineering,
With their herpes, their Strike Hard policies
Gone...Phoof...Khallas…
Finito!

In my dreams I see three MIGs
Flying over Beijing
Bombing to rubble
The entire Zhongnanhai compound

While during the day I paint
The walls, the parapets, the windows
In the scorching sun of New Mexico
My *juru*² dangling from my neck

In my dreams I see three MIGs
Flying over Beijing

Bombing to rubble
The entire Zhongnanhai compound

¹ independence
² a coral bead worn by Tibetans

Mother
Tsamchoe Dolma

She is there at last
In tears,
Stretching arms
That call me to her.
With revived love
She-mama,
Wishes to call me now
And tell me how much she cares
Deep down,
With love she whispers,
Shouts,
Screams,
And then wails.
But they never reach me...
There is the ocean of distance
And I am miles apart from her.
I try to see through her,
Into the dark labyrinth
Of her heart,
I plead for a tear
And a sigh,
But neither seems to acquiesce!
I, with my helplessness,
And she, with her endless despair,
The ocean of distance
And the eternity of pain,
Of longings,

But again she pulls herself to me,
Cold wrinkled hands
 Feeling for me,
Then she covers me with wet kisses
And drenches my soul,
 With a flood of tears
And believe me,
She smiles through them!
But again,
Relapses into a mournful gloom
A long sigh
And a piercing pause
Then close to my heart she comes,
Sends down a whisper,
A long desperate call
And they do reach me then!
There is the ocean of distance
And I'm miles apart from her,
But she is always there
Deep within my heart.

<u>Footnote</u>: With many children sent from Tibet into exile for schooling, separation from parents is commonplace.

A Voice
Tsamchoe Dolma

Something inside me calls,
Brushes aside my senses
And takes me to depths,
Where no one can reach.
Something inside me pains.
But I know not why...
I walk up high hills
And seek moments of silence,
 But I only know,
Something inside me hurts.
It can't be that I laugh,
Or smile, for reasons unknown,
It can't be that I cry,
For that something is still unknown.

Freedom
Tsamchoe Dolma

Its night again....
The sky is jewelled with the stars.
And the moon fully attired.
The wind in the trees, their branches
Dancing,
Yet I am alone, alone in my iron cage.
I see no light though I hear
And I desire to be in the open night...
To fly, far, far away,
To reach out to the sky
To feel the soft wind,
Yet I can't...
The hours in the cage seem years
The moon I see is far away
Yet not vanishing,
I long to dream in the open sky,
I long to feel the beauty of night,
Yet I can't...

It's day again...
The sky's so blue, the sun's so full!
Yet I don't feel its warmth,
My friends are on their wings,
Yet mine is out of use
I'm locked, barred and ruined,
I try to see the world I hear is beautiful,
Yet only the iron barred cage do I see,

I direct my scream heavenward,
Yet a solitary echo do I hear.
My world is my cage.
Solitude, my only friend
For I'm but a barred bird,
Cut off from the freedom I long for.

Nangsel
Tsamchoe Dolma

She trotted down the muddy lane
Her boots soiled and legs in pain,
She held her dolly to her arms
The penny precious tight in her palms,
She sang her rhymes on and on
As she trotted down and down,
The rains did platter
But it did not matter,
For Nangsel would not care
Except for the candies so rare,
One for Pala, one for Amala,
One for Zeky and one for Peky
One for the sad boy
Who lost his toy,
One each for her buddies,
Who love those candies.

They Are Still Too Young
Tsamchoe Dolma

They are a dozen or more
but still less,
Their wings are strong
But not ready for flight,
They are my own
but they need recognition,
They are desperate to fly,
but I restrain,
They are still young
and I know it by my heart,
They speak words
which only I understand,
They are my soul mates
reflection of my emotions,
They bring me tears
but soothe my soul,
They are still innocent
unaware of the world,
They tell me they are ready
I'm afraid they are not.
They still have to grow
in size and depth,
They are what I feed
with joy and sombre,
They always ask for liberty,
They want to take off
and soar high...

They want to give wings
to my dreams,
They say,
"Mother, we will do you proud"
They say,
"Mother, expose us to the world"
They, my passion
my silent poems,
They say it
but they are still too young.

Love Story of the Snail Queen
Tsamchoe Dolma

I met the snail queen yesterday.
She had a new crown on.
She led me in her palace.
Down into the earth.
She offered me drinks and meals.
She let me play her golden harp.
A hundred snail maids entertained me,
But the snail queen looked sad…
"Your majesty," I then asked.
"Why this gloom on your pretty face?"
She shed a silent tear then
And led me to her private park
Where beside a tomb she knelt
And thus related,
" The air was wet and wonderful,
 It was the snail-ball last monsoon,
And I met a charming snail prince.
The smartest antenna he had
And I did fall for him!
We danced till the moonlights were gone.
We roamed the snail city arm in arm.
And that golden harp he gave me then
(The snail tradition to ask to be wed)
The monsoon feast was our wedding day.
And never more happy were we then!
My maids got me ready.
They curled my antenna,

Coloured my shell
And with this new crown I was adorned.
Wedding bells had filled the air.
And the feast had just begun.
But the prince did not turn up!
The scouts traced him everywhere
They blew the emergency horn,
They put special receptors on
And after hours of search, up and down,
They finally brought his distorted corpse,
While on his way to the wedding,
Two giant feet had squashed him twice!
My love story,
The usual snail-story,
Had just come to an end."

A Whisper
Tsamchoe Dolma

It's not a pledge made
Neither dreams woven
And then destroyed,
Nor imaginations reflected
And then vanished,
Not pleasant memories cherished.
It's not even a breeze that kissed
And left someone blushed,
Not a divine touch that blessed
Nor a sight that one glance delighted
No way a smile that brightened,
Not even a word said
It's just a whisper that rippled
Away and away …
And then vanished.

Destination...Heart
Tsamchoe Dolma

All set for the journey,
'Love', alone proceeded.
"The trip is long,
May I come along?"
'Desire' meekly asked.
'Love' nodded in a daze.
'Passion' too peeped in then
And 'Lust' forced in to join.
The journey was a pleasure then,
Until 'Pain' insisted he come along.
How can poor 'Love' deny?
The town of 'Greed' was not far then
And he, with his pot-belly demanded.
"Journey to the paradise
And I am not invited?"
So marched together,
The distant crew.
'Love' loathed the company then
And began to shed a tear.
But uncle 'Ego' popped in then
And casually wiped the drop,
Lest no one see it fall.
"Without me, the journey isn't complete."
He thus roared.
'Love' wasn't anymore happy then.
And when after days,
They reached their destination... heart,

The closed gate boldly read.
"Private Residence, Mr. Hatred.
All except, 'Love' is accepted".

Silent Souls
Tsamchoe Dolma

Silent souls swelled with feeling
Yet concealing with a naked veil,
Holding back the tears until there is a corner
Pushing away the emotions that never leave,
For pride reigns in these mighty kingdoms
And separate souls instead of bridging,
Killing and piercing, it commands
Little troops of words that shatter
Silent souls blossoming into love.

Stolen Moments of Life
Tsamchoe Dolma

A few stolen moments
That is just mine,
A lone sail and a sun set for eternity
Are all that I need,
A dusky moor and a sober sky,
A wild canvas of landscape
Bare but beautiful,
A lone grazer on a carpet of marsh
A few splashes of waves…
Are all that I seek,
A silent kiss of a salty breeze
A gentle touch of an open sea
A few stolen moments
For lifetime to go.

Twilight's Delight
Tsamchoe Dolma

Shy drizzles and a shimmering pond
Await the glow of the twilight king,
Clouds swing on lofty heights,
Wind murmurs a slurry tune.
And so dance the autumn leaves
To and fro, down and down,
Old blossom princesses descend their throne
And bless the ground with a carpet of fragrance,
Clip-clop, clip-clop, the droplets drum,
Somewhere the nightingales sing...
And owls croon their motherly note
Welcoming the nature's delight.
Gently and silently
Twilight kisses his beloved queen
And she blushes in crimson shades,
While the breeze starts whispering
Clouds swing a little more,
So do the autumn leaves in wanton glee,
Rustles to note the miraculous merge
And seem to say,
'Twilight, Twilight, thy bride is beautiful!'

The Mother Cuckoo
Tsamchoe Dolma

The mist was gone somewhere in the depth of the valley
The shower left a sweet scent on the mushy earth,
The wind was calm in the serenity of the air
And the mother cuckoo was still on the rain-washed tree,
Cooing all day long as if her song would never die,
I never heard a lyric so full of pain, so melancholic
That a dark heavy lump squeezed by my throat,
Then the bliss of the vicinity bade a reluctant farewell
And the echo of the song seeped within my soul;
She seemed to whimper, painful tears of desperation
She seemed to give the sad news from far beyond,
But the meaning try hard I could not understand,
I never heard a lyric so full of pain, so melancholic
That the lump grew and grew as if it would never die,
Then for one last time she brushed her rain soaked fur
And I thought about the forbidden land she left behind,
A solitary feather swung from her withered wings
And then the mother cuckoo was no longer to be seen.

Lone-1
Bhuchung D. Sonam

World, so full of people
Each one lonely within,
Strives to find that SOMEONE
Who fits their distorted ideals,
While the years go passing by,
We accumulate chains of wrinkles
Each one a sad tale,
A failed love, a broken dream.

World, so full of people
Each one a lonesome soul
Basks in the fading rays of life,
Desires this, hopes that,
We accumulate pangs of failure
Each one filed behind another
Like dunes of desert sand
that keep repeating ... endlessly.

From a Prison Diary
Bhuchung D. Sonam

Through my tainted glass
I can see the sky bluer,
But then, I am a comic crestfallen prisoner
Swathed in red jingoistic jargon,
Restlessly churned in the desolate prison yard,
"Bayonets speak louder than words!
Nails that stick out will be hammered down!"
I once was a nail that stuck out
I still am a nail, head smashed through,
My voiceless incoherency supersedes
        Agonies of hunger,
        Chills of fear,
        Cries for freedom,
        Fear of reprisal,
        Grumbles of inmates…

Through my mind, saturated with conflicts
Amidst a web of cumulative cries,
I can hear myself within me,
Making clarion calls for a million things.
I repress them, I suppress them,
Lest bayonets get the better of me.

In the clouded eyes of the marching guards
I am just another insane inmate.
In my dossier with PSB[1],
I could be anything they fancy,

> A splittist agent
> Of the Dalai clique,
> A counter revolutionary,
> An enemy of the Motherland…

In the annals of the freedom struggle
I am one of the faceless, nameless entities,
Who choke on something that they believe in,
Something they are willing to die for.
> A spacious freedom
> A precious dignity
> The bluest sky
> The whitest snow.

From my grilled prison window
I can see the silhouettes of the guards,
Armed to the teeth, brute force pronounced,
I am caged…
But they cannot control my thoughts.
> My expanding ideas
> My quest for freedom
> My silent songs.

I am a comic crestfallen prisoner
Bayonets are stronger than words
    for now, at least.

---

[1] China's Public Security Bureau police

Dylan, Me and Robin Hood
Bhuchung D. Sonam

On the Friendship road
We travel writing a note
Dylan, me and Robin Hood,
Roasted barley for our food,
Dylan twangs his six-string guitar,
It sounds much like a sitar,
Me the bad little boy
Fumbles with a baby toy,
Robin waves his mighty bow
So to make the Chinese bow,
Thousand eyes watch us parade,
Though we aren't on a visit so state,
There is something in these eyes
That we could not see,
Something in the air
That we could not feel,
A melancholic tune from an untuned *da.nyen*[1],
A butter lamp left half burnt
A fragile mind shaken out of tune,
A virgin land trembled by the marching boots,
A civilization being ripped apart.

[1] Tibetan lute

Dandelions of Tibet
Bhuchung D. Sonam

They were in full foliage
The dandelions of Tibet,
When the hail stormed
Maiming all that there was,
Each yellow petal estranged
From the mother bud,
Roam aimless in strange meadows
Where they rot unknown and unclaimed.

Of Death and Peace
Bhuchung D. Sonam

Now that the dust has settled
And the dead not forgotten quite
Music flowed from his *da.nyen*[1]
Ensnared by nostalgia ...
The memories of the years
Sweetly stolen by sunny days.

When he got married four
And half decades ago
Dazzled by the mundane pleasure
Death was but a distant thought.

During his first visit to the monastery
At his wife's first pregnancy
He became aware of impermanence
As an old *geshe*[2] serenely spoke
Sipping his butter tea.

Rejoicing the birth of his eldest son
He strummed his *da.nyen*
Producing melody that lingered
Danced to by the women folk – old and young
Envied by the men
He prevailed; so did his wealth
Cattle multiplied, more sons followed.

On the day of his wife's death

The diaphanous sky poured.
It was Sunday.
Geshe shook his head while
Performing the astrological calculation for the dead
"Nine miniature human figures must be buried
in nine holes with a butter lamp on each" he said.

The body was kept in the house for three days facing southeast
A white *tsa.tsa*³ on the chest and
*Hrî*⁴ mantra written on paper on the forehead
By the time they took her she was covered in white scarves.

The following seven weeks were filled with prayers
And smoke that arose from the *sûr*⁵
A *thangka*⁶ of Green Tara was commissioned at an exorbitant price
She will be reborn, the calculation said, in the realm of the gods

The butter lamps still burn though in reduced number
One thousand of them burnt on the forty ninth
The day she finally travelled to the higher realm.

Now that the dust has settled
And the dead not forgotten quite
Music flowed from his *da.nyen*
Notes culminating to a dirge…
He looked beyond and behind

The life that passed on the other side of the window
His heart bled inside – but no blood oozed

Then discarding his *da.nyen* forever
Behind the door that creaked every day
He clutched his grandfather's rosary
And amidst the fragrance of his declining years
– He found peace.

---

[1] Tibetan lute
[2] The highest monastic degree in Tibetan Buddhist Philosophy
[3] miniature images of buddhas, deities or stupas, moulded of clay
[4] a mystical word meaning essence or substance
[5] Tibetan ritual offering by burning flour mixed with sacred substances to nourish the *bardo* consciousness and placate hungry ghosts
[6] a traditional Tibetan scroll painting mounted on silk brocade

Song of an Old Tibetan
Bhuchung D. Sonam

I sing for all things dead and alive
For all things moving and still
For all moms who cry for their faraway sons,
For dear moms who laugh with their nearby daughters
I sing for all fathers – strict watch dogs
For their scared craving maidens
And young men for their fathomless passion for flesh,
I sing for my compatriots
…the kindred souls
…restless spirits,
I sing for the young buds
For their struggle to be full fledged flowers
For flowers that age with honey bees,
For butterflies and their colourful wings,
Green grasshoppers for their ceaseless hops,
I sing for, myself, the traveller
The ever wandering vagabond,
Chased from where I belong
Eluded by promises and hopes
Belonging to a vaunted Diaspora
That fights from atop a beautiful hill,
And for all travellers with no destination
For all fights fought and yet to fight
For the lost chord unfound
For the trial that rises upward
For the revised spirit
For gentler hearts

For the Promised Land
The snow sunk upland
Closer to where I want to die.

India – I See It Soon Depart
Tenzin Trinley

This land of the teeming multitude
Is not ours though we dwell
For decades in agonies of dreams...
Faintly I see — our destiny
A blurred silhouette
Of freedom perhaps,
With its trail trailing
On to the land of a hundred sons,
From where we must leave
Not to decay in conceited certitude

And India, I see it soon depart
To the land of tantalizing vistas
To trace footprints of our forefathers,
To revive our childhood memories
Of valleys and pastures
Of chimes and chants

Here we came to read our history
To reaffirm pride in our root
To reassert our pledge for freedom,
And India, I see it soon depart
In chimes of freedom
And cry of victory.

Ode to Dhondup Gyal
Kalsang Wangdu

Passing over the lofty mountains
fluttering prayer flags,
the highland gale carried
an unparalleled melody of shepherd's flute,
He sings the song thou hath long ago sung,
boughs bowed, rivulets skipped a breath
In a poignant moment I hearken to
thy immense songs of glowing
beauties and wisdoms,

Thou gave warmth to the snow
and the height to the Everest,
But when thy soaring wings
reached sky...and touched the stars,
thou confront a party... a people
who held back thy breath
In the pain of eternal silence.

Oh!! Dhondup Gyal...
Death hath not done to you,
for thy verses are full of life
And transcend the earthly
bound of time and space,
Snows bore thy indelible marks
even the winds call thy name
Youth of Tibet are on their feet
to move mountains,

And to march towards freedom
thou shall now rest in complete peace
on the cosy lap of the eternal king.
Wake up sometimes and watch
the gallant forward march
of the doughty youth of Tibet.

Footnote: Dhondup Gyal (1953-1985) was born in Gurong Phuba in Amdo, north-eastern Tibet. He was a prolific author and poet who devised the new style (Tib. *snyan ngag gsar pa*) of Tibetan poetry. For more on D. Gyal's work see Lungta vol. 9, winter 1995 and Lungta vol. 12, summer 1999, Amnye Machen Institute, Dharamshala, India.

A Blind Farmer?
Ugen Choephel

Slowly and silently the sun peeps
Over snow-capped high eastern peaks,
Blessing with its infinite golden threads
Through the window upon a farmer's breads.

Its warmth on mountains of silver snow,
Melts the blanket to let it flow
Into young winding rivulets to the fields,
Where the farmer labours for the yield.

Its rhythmic alarm wakes each dreaming plant
From the cold dark night – rejuvenated,
Resumes their gentle growth process,
Thus reassures the farmer's gradual progress.

With its touch from the crust of ocean,
Sips up moist for clouds' passion,
To rain should the cloud fail
Or in angst does it hail?
To great a peril does the farmer derail.

Drenched in sweat the peasant looks up
Smiles at the cloud and heaves a sigh,
Questions the sun with look so evil,
'Why glare so hard – you hot devil?'

The Freedom Song
Thupten N. Chakrishar

Let me sing a song
The rhythm belongs to the mountains
The words to the green pastures.

>Let me sing a song
>A song of freedom
>I cannot sing my own land.

I do not want to be accurate
But it was in the middle of 1959,
I cannot tell you in detail
They killed my father.

>I ask you for no help
>I have done that a million times,
>I accept no compromise
>What is mine is rightfully mine.

Liberation was what they said
Sufferings are all we paid.
Universal brotherhood is what we hear
But never seen I must swear.

>Do you seek happiness? I ask
>As I seek in every task.
>Decades ago they snatched my happiness
>Want to bring back but I am helpless.

There are parts where the sun don't shine
With our blood now they dine,
This is the right time to act
Lest the whole civilization vanishes.

> The world is not listening
> My friends are just pretending.
> You may be waiting for something
> My brothers are dying.

Save Tibet, I must request
For long I cannot hold
My sisters are being sold.

> You can make a difference
> A light within ignorance,
> You can help free Tibet – just join me
> Family of a better world you can be.

Rise! Don't wait
Help me sing this freedom song
"Freedom is not everything, it is the only thing".

My Last Wish
Thupten N. Chakrishar

Oh! My friends
Pierce my eyes with a sword
for I can no longer see my Mother suffer,
curse me for I cannot save her.

Cut my arms for they are useless
bonded with laws of the world.
Cut my legs for they are fettered
I cannot walk to my Mother.

Take my tongue with a hot blade
because my voice disappears
in the mist of communist China.

Chop away my ear lobes
for they are my problem
I cannot hear the cries of my Mother.

But when I die, my dear friends
cut my head as my last wish
and present it to the UN
so that they will realize
that the spirit never dies.

Together
Thupten N. Chakrishar

Sun
Clouds
Birds
Mountains
Trees
River
Flowers
A beautiful house...
You
Me
Alone
Together
Forever...

The Fallen Leaf
Thupten N. Chakrishar

Flowers bloomed in spring
the trees were green,
everything seemed beautiful
as it had never been.
The wind had a rhythm
a song did they sing,
The waves did they splash
sweet to the ears,
Birds flew freely
Ignoring the borders of the world,
Roses bloomed full
As they murmured softly in the air,
Time rolled by
memories slipped,
Flowers began to fade,
Seasons rolled,
Leaves fell
on the dry earth...
But never did she return
And I am the fallen leaf.

A Pledge
Thupten N. Chakrishar

Before I fade away
I will find a way,
To make you FREE...
Wait for me MOTHER
I will set you FREE.

A Dry Leaf
Namgyal Phuntsok

Like a dry leaf, my heart crumbles
Within your tiny grasp,
Remember ...
'One should let one's emotion go'
You told me last Valentine.

Obeying you I walked along your path
with you at the other end
hands wide open,
twinkle in your eyes
a deep ocean of mystery.

Like an escort you led me
to a dark hollow end,
I crawled like a baby,
bruises on my knees
an undying struggle.

How kind of you to prove me wrong,
You are the victor and I the loser
with my love in your palm
ready to be crumbled like a dry leaf

Stone Boy's Confession
Namgyal Phuntsok

I live in a paradise of my own
where no beautiful dreams come true,
Days and nights are of no different
only empty dreams embedded in my heart.
I have no dear and near ones,
people call me an idiot
a name I love to hate,
Children giggle at me
adults make fun of me,
At times I wonder if I am
one of God's children,
Sometimes I wonder
if I am one of their funny jokes,
I live in a paradise
a paradise of my own.

The Call
Namgyal Phuntsok

a few words to say
a few promises to keep,
summer seems to pale
but the promises still young
like the first snowflake on your cheek,
blue sky promises a fall
a ride into the stationed clouds,
the last leaf on the tree
promises soon to return,
the dying sun promises a new dawn,
folding petals promise
to bloom again, to radiate love,
but ignores the one who is in pain
one who is in complete solitude,
waiting for his promised love...
his eyes wide open,
tired but hopeful,
hopeful that she will keep
her promise of
life full of love and laughter,
Like a little boy building a sand castle
hoping it will remain forever,
he weeps and waits ... ever hopeful
that one day she will come to him
his love ...to bloom in all seasons.

Thriving in the Flames
Namgyal Phuntsok

I am tired being on somebody else's land
I am tired with the rallies and strikes I
participated
I waited till this age to be back home
And to feel the crisp air of my native land
Since the waiting alone isn't enough
I gave all I had – my own self… my own life
hoping my people will learn something.
Here in exile new trends are making their hold
This isn't my culture, my real identity
Back there at home, a single call for Independence
Mouths gagged and subjected to solitary confinement
No options left, they look for us with hope
Where at least we have the freedom of expression
Time calls for a change – a dramatic change
Let's be practical rather than leaning on options
I am tired of being on somebody else's land
I am tired of rallies and strikes I
Participated…
I waited till this age to be back home
And to feel the crisp air of my native land
Since the waiting alone isn't enough
I gave all I had – my own self… my own life
hoping my people will learn something

I Have Aged
Tenzin Palzom

I fall on the pavement
Or into the water,
I travel places
A child's toy
An ant's boat,
I fly …
When the wind falls in love with me
And carries me to his home
Over the horizon,
I sing
A flute for the shepherd's son,
I die
Beneath your shoes crushed
Or burnt in your backyard,
I am not a phoenix
Nor am I a dragon
I am only an aged dry leaf.

Footnote: Tenzin Palzom is a seventh grade student of Tibetan Children's Village school, Dharamshala. This poem was first published in *Students' Forum* 2003.

Caveat
Sherab W. Choephel

Death laughs in your eyes
Spits on your face,
Resides in your veins,
He sees you shadowless ...
You live on a toss – head or tail?

Your laugh is a hollow shout
Amplified conceit of a dying soul,
You look in the rear mirror
And he gives a death smile.

You are dying – my pal
And I sing your dirge.

Tibet is My Destination
Anonymous

Tibet is my destiny
Not far can I see.
Fists in the air
slogans on the rise,
How long can this last?
And how many are we
who are willing to die?
Sad is the day
When my parents say
"We will never see Tibet free"
Fearful I am
of the buds of today,
Will they ever blossom
into glory of tomorrow?
Or will they perish
in the sorrowful heat of the noon?
Proud as I am
To be a full-blooded Tibetan,
But leaders who inspire
are far and few,
Intensely I yearn to see Tibet free
Long I wish for leaders to lead...
INDEPENDENCE is my quest
AUTONOMY is their lame offer.
My dictum is to fight
to the last DROP OF BLOOD.
Truly I am

an alien in an alien soil,
materially lured I am
to the shores of America.
but FREEDOM is my DIGNITY
and TIBET – my DESTINATION.

Is It Snowing In Tibet?
Wongchen Tsering

Is it snowing in my motherland?
I thought between hesitation and yearning
Snow – lifeline of my generation
Snow – protector of my land
Snow, in you I have discovered compassion
when I am so far from you,
Snow – mind of a warrior race
Snow – eye of the spirited Tibetans
Snow – lasting hero in the land of darkness.

Is it snowing in my motherland?
I thought between hesitation and yearning
Snow, in you I have discovered beauty
Snow, you stay forever high and pure
watering the desolate Jhang Thang
Snow – rejuvenating nectar of my mind
Snow – lighting butter lamp in my heart
Snow – you are the poetry of our people.
Snow, in you I seek my dreams
Snow, in your name I write my poetry.
Is it snowing in my motherland?
I thought between hesitation and yearning.

Emptiness
Tsering Dolkar

Starlit nights are here again
maybe this time to stay forever,
I'm drunk with the scent of life
though not sweet but I love it,
Staring ahead into the space
which is mine in some vague ways,
Its beauty lies in its nothingness...
Emptiness is peace,
Emptiness is a friend
So much more seductive
than giant echoes,
With emptiness I retire
into that space meant for me....

Emptiness Again
Gur Gyal

Starry nights are here again,
But I am aware its only a mirage,
Countless stars cleaved and burned,
Like all phenomena, they too retire into nothingness
thus consuming my craving in their eternity.
I too was drunk with the scent of life
Yet by recognizing the impermanence of all phenomena,
tastes have reduced to tastelessness,
love and hate have lost their meanings,
Absorbed in the bliss of non conceptual mind
my heart sings
I fathom the true nature of mind,
And the self that I project
is but an innate emptiness
where Karma manifest,
knowing this gives me primordial bliss,
And by realizing this true nature of mind
nothing seduces my mind,
When subjects and objects are examined,
all appearances are
but echoes of emptiness,
knowing this,
I retire into the blissful emptiness of my mind.

Cry Tibet
Gur Gyal

Cry Tibet! My beloved Fatherland, Cry!
Another of your brave sons has fallen.
Yet again, another bastion of freedom has fallen.
Soon your children will gather with tumultuous voices,
In grief beat their breasts.
Hypocrites talk of defending your honour
while charlatans seek your cheerless hours,
They talk with their voices raised
pledges they offer of freeing you.
While innocents yearn for martyrdom
the scheming few talk of compromising on you

Cry Tibet! My beloved Fatherland, Cry!
It is your children who have let you down,
Chasing self-interest and shallow beliefs
they left you in shame and dishonour.
Upon the gilded foreign shores
They chant a few half-hearted slogans
After the dust of this frenzy has settled
they will forget you again
As your true sons have fallen and forgotten
your fate again recedes into oblivion.

Cry Tibet! My beloved Fatherland, Cry!
Another of your brave sons has fallen.
Cry Tibet! My beloved Fatherland, Cry!
Yet again, another bastion of freedom has fallen.

Shambhala
Dhargyal Tsering

Along a dark tunnel I walk
Not knowing where it leads,
Dampness makes me sneeze
my body aches.
A lamp glows at the far end
a sign of hope
a sign of survival
and then
Shambhala beams in front of me
and I become.

The View
Pema Tenzin

the view from
Kopan hill
is impermanent

the view from
leopard field
absorbs all thoughts

the view from
the grassy seat
dissolves into mist

the view
of mind
is emptiness.

Three Things I Wait For...
Dawa Woeser

I wait for freedom every month…every year
But it never seems to come
I have a precious human life
But I am chased into another land
So I do not like to live long on this earth.

I wait to see my parents every day…every night
But a meeting never takes place
Where I live now
Even the honey tastes stale
So I do not like to stay long in this alien land.

I wait for my beloved
But she never comes
Even if playing with angels in heaven
The soul within me is empty
So I do not like to live on this earth.

Footnote: Dawa Woeser is a sixth grade student of Tibetan Transit School, Dharamshala. This poem was first published in the annual school magazine, *The New Horizon*, Issue 3, 2001.

Don't be Afraid Mother
Kathup Tsering

Don't be afraid, mother
my dear delicate mother

Mother...
The soul of the snow
walks alone on the dark path
where freedom eludes

Don't be afraid, mother
though the hopes fail
the sky falls
wind blows
rivers flow
and upon the fresh soft snow
I see your tender footprints

Don't be afraid, mother
should the storms rise
I will stand for you
on the snowy road
the spirit of your vision rings
should hurdles arise
I will lay myself
to protect your legacy

Don't be afraid, mother
the mind closes

the heart freezes
    the life ceases
in the Land of sorrow (Snow)
     yet I sing
  the songs of freedom
as your vision never quivers

 Don't be afraid, mother
   as the rain still falls
  the spring forth cometh
FREEDOM…surely will resound.

Barkhor
Kathup Tsering

Darkness descends
From the sky
Ere sunset
And wraps Barkhor...

Machine guns
Like thunder's echo
bodies scatter
Souls shatter
On the narrow path of Barkhor

The broken prayer-wheel
still turns
In the hand of an old mother
Who murmurs
The last breath of life.

The devilish bullets
Pierce the hearts
of men, women and children
Around the Barkhor
In the dusk of the bloody day
Arise voices ...of freedom
bare hands against the machine guns.

From that day
Fathers detained

Incarcerated in cells
Mothers driven beyond sanity
Little homes broken apart
orphaned children beg
In the streets of Barkhor

Behold the holy city
The hell unleashed upon
Darkness descend
From the sky
ere the sunset
And shrouds Barkhor
in an envelope of misery.

Footnote: Barkhor is the inner circular road in Lhasa which goes around Tsuglakhang and is a major market

In This Life I Saw
Kathup Tsering

a man
devoid of limbs
lying on the ground
a headless horse
its hair bristled
for fear of the wind
in this life I saw.

a soldier
dead in the battlefield
a broken gun upon his head
a gun
that fell him down
in this life I saw.

a child
struggled across the snow-mountains
left his parent back home
over the snowy pass
he lost his toes
in this life I saw

The Majestic Himalayas
Cherin' Norbu

Behold thy eyes
see the colossal Himalayas
Standing before me so silently
For a moment the frozen peaks
Overwhelm me.

In solitude
Upon the cold starry skies
The silence engulfs me
When only the cold wind
Sings over the naked snow.

I stand at the threshold
of the void mystic Himalayas
towering in the horizon so pride
The majestic Himalayas…
I salute your silence and enormity.

Dreams
Tenzin Gelek

I had a dream of a world so free,
Where all strive for happiness and glee.
I had a dream of people so pleasant,
Their kindness does heaven embarrass.
I had a dream of water so pure,
The taste of which does many a cure.
I had a dream of mountains so high
Standing tall and white, kissing the sky.
I had a dream of my country deserted and bemused,
And tears flowed from my shaken and bruised heart.
To the people of the world I ask
What is it that they desire the most?
Is it the 'treasures of the world?'
For me freedom cannot be measured in gold.
Only can freedom give me 'my peace of mind'
As I rummage my soul 'Free Tibet' is all I find.

Footnote: This poem was inspired by the famous speech "I have a dream…" by the black American civil rights activist, Martin Luther King.

Romancing the Night
Tenzin Gelek

Yet another day passes, yet another night sleeps
In slurry of dreams, love comes in heaps.
Yet another face, yet another fantasy
A passionate storm rides high over me.
Wild and hazy, yet a beautiful sight,
A lonely heart romancing the night.
A part of me thinks its deep down insane,
But another part wishes for that night again.
I wait the night anticipating the hidden
Craving for passion like a fruit forbidden,
Curiosity on my mind taking a flight
With my lonely heart romancing the night.
As the evening passes, I flirt the twilight away
When the night arrived there was little left to say,
A few may assume I am paranoid,
Yet I have no time for an argument,
For this night stands only till the morning light.
So, let leave my lonely heart, romancing the night.

Unfulfilled Promises
Tenzin Gelek

I was promised a birth
  On the Roof of the World,
My playfield – the high mountains
  My endeavour – to roam across the Jhang Thang.

To wake up to the soulful hymns
  And the re-vibrating prayer gong.
Breathing the free air of my land
  A place where I belong.

A breakfast of *tsampa* and butter tea
Herding the majestic yaks and sheep,
  Along the rivers and over the meadows.

Archery on galloping horses,
  I was promised – I would play.
An occasional toast of *chang*,
  Followed by a round *"Tashi Shapdro"*[1]

Above all, I was promised a land of my own
  But I was born in an alien country
On a loaned plot of land.

Tagged as a refugee
Growing up on a snowless land,
Who has stolen my promises?

---

[1] a type of traditional Tibetan dance meaning 'auspicious dance'

Mr. Fart
Tshering Dorjee

It mingles and mingles for toxic
Worthy to squeeze for departure,
Through varying sounds
from bong, ping, phoos
to reck, doom, taang,
it comes out for a mission.
Noisy ones are barking dogs
that seldom bite
simple and silent are the ones
that create hostility.
Sneeringly the owner asks
"Did you fart?" his face
Full of innocence,

"God" is the expression
"Phooh" is the dispersing warning
everybody spreads and leaving
the owner of the human product
phoohingly and shame facedly
still disclaiming any knowledge
of the unknown culprit.

Gendun Choephel Wailing from Nangtse Shar Prison
Bhuchung D. Sonam

Loose …gone down
Crack … pulled out
Madness … forced upon me
I am a jellyfish
But I couldn't slip through them
I am the precious one
But I have no strength to stand
Nor will to go forward
I am a dead fish
No motion anywhere
I am an anti-anti
My worth worthless
I am the only kind
I am sequestered
I am a white crow
They see me black
Black as their eyeballs
I am a black sheep
But I gave *White Annals*
I am a rare kind
I am a wild flower
Tamed but untamed
I am lucky
Dying in Potala Palace
Grown old before time
Strength undiscovered
I am dying growing
Take care of my books – They are all I have…

About the Poets

Gendun Choephel (1905–1951) was undoubtedly the most iconoclastic and versatile Tibetan scholar of the twentieth century. Besides his extensive writings on Tibetan history, culture and religion, he was, perhaps, the first Tibetan ever to write poetry in English. His many works include *White Annals: The Political History of Great Tibet*, *A Guide to Sacred Places in India*, *An Ornament to Nagarjuna's Intention: Essential Points of Madyhamaka* and *The Blue Annals* in collaboration with George N. Roerich. He died at the age of 47 shortly after the Chinese invasion.

Chögyam Trungpa (1939–1987) was born in Kham, eastern Tibet, and was recognized as the XI Trungpa Tulku of Surmang group of monasteries by the XVI Gyalwa Karmapa. After the Chinese occupation of Tibet, he escaped into exile and became a leading spiritual guide to westerners, first in Scotland and later in America. Meditation master, scholar, artist and poet Trungpa founded Naropa Insititute in Boulder, Colorado, including the Jack Kerouac School of Poetics. His numerous best-selling works include *Cutting Through Spiritual Materialism*, *Myth of Freedom*, *Meditation in Action*, *First Thought Best Thought* and *Crazy Wisdom*.

Lhasang Tsering was born in Tibet and bought into exile at a young age. In 1972, giving up an opportunity to study medicine in the US, he joined the armed Tibetan resistance force, who were then operating from Mustang, Nepal. He was later President of Tibetan Youth Congress and a founding director of Amnye Machen Institute. Lhasang, an outspoken and ardent advocate for Tibetan independence and a passionate lover of literature, currently runs Bookworm—a bookshop in Dharamshala – with his wife.

K. Dhondup (1952–1995) was born in Rupin Gang of upper Dromo, Tibet. After graduating from St. Joseph's College, Darjeeling, he joined the Library of Tibetan Works and Archives, Dharamshala. He was a poet, historian and a journalist. His works include *Songs of the Sixth Dalai Lama*, *The Water-Horse and Other Years: a history of 17th and 18th century Tibet* and *The Water-Birds and Other Years: a history of the 13th Dalai Lama and after*. He passed away on May 7, 1995 in New Delhi.

Gyalpo Tsering completed his schooling from the prestigious Dr. Graham's Homes in Kalimpong. In 1973 he left his teaching job at the Tibetan Children's Village school to join the Tibetan resistance – then operating from Mustang, in western Nepal. Later he also worked at the Information and Publicity Office of H. H. the Dalai Lama (now the Department of Information and International Relations, DIIR). Gyalpo has now settled in Canada.

Ngodup Paljor (1948–1988) was a "secretary to mountains" who walked the mountains and crossed vast cultural divides. His love for hiking mountains superseded nothing and he wrote poems while drinking Tibetan tea near noisy streams. He walked over a bridge from the highlands of Western

Tibet to a life in Alaska's largest city. Along the way he was a refugee, a monk and a student and was fluent in Tibetan, Hindi, Sanskrit, Pali, Thai and English. He served as a translator for His Holiness the Dalai Lama and was an assistant professor of Tibetan studies at the University of Hawaii. He founded The Alaska Tibet Committee and Khawachen Dharma Centre to promote Tibetan culture. Paljor died as a result of an accident at the Port of Anchorage, while working as a longshoreman on October 25, 1988. He was around forty years old.

Tsoltim N. Shakabpa was born in Lhasa, Tibet in 1943. He was educated in Tibet, India and US and had worked for the Tibetan Government-in-Exile in India. He was diagnosed with stomach cancer in 1993 and had a debilitating stroke in 1999. But he battled these setbacks and his first book of poems RECORDS DÕUN TIBETA was translated and published in the Catalan language by the prestigious Pages Editors. In 2002, he received the EDITORÕS CHOICE AWARD for Outstanding Achievement in Poetry from the International Library of Poetry. Mr. Shakabpa's second new book of poems *Recollections of a Tibetan* was published by Publish America in the US. He is the Executive Director of Tsepon Wangchuk Deden Shakabpa Memorial Foundation and is an advocate for the independence of Tibet.

Tenzing Sonam was born in 1959 in Darjeeling, India. After graduating from Delhi University, he worked for a year in the Tibetan Government-in-Exile in Dharamshala. He then led a peripatetic life for a few years, doing a variety of odd jobs in Switzerland, New York, Scottsdale and Los Angeles before fetching up at the Graduate School of Journalism at the University of California, Berkeley, where he specialized in documentary filmmaking. He was a founder-member of the Bay Area Friends of Tibet. He is a writer and along with his wife and filmmaking partner, Ritu Sarin, runs White Crane Films, which has specialized in films on Tibetan subjects. He is currently based in Delhi. The poems in this collection were written when he was 19 years old.

G. C. (Gendun Choephel April 15, 1964 – October 10, 1992) was born in Dharamshala and studied in Tibetan Children's Village school. He was something of an enigma amongst his small circle of friends – a man who loved songs and fathomed their deeper meanings. But he was, as his wife T. R. Choephel wrote, "a youth to fame and fortune unknown/ fair signs frowned on his humble birth/and he gave misery all he had a – tear". He lived a short, but tumultuous life of dreams, drugs, desperation and rift. When he died under mysterious circumstances, all he left behind was a dark-blue diary full of verses reflecting his love for Tibet and an ounce of imaginings.

Topden Tsering, born in Dharamshala, a small town in North India, is the former the editor of *Tibetan Bulletin*. He is presently the President of San Francisco Tibetan Youth Congress. He divides his time between Free Tibet activism, his interest in graphic designing and his passion for literature. He can be reached at stopden@yahoo.co.uk

Tenzin Tsundue is a writer-activist born to a refugee family in Manali, North India. After graduating from Loyola College, Chennai, he received MA from University of Mumbai. He is the author of two poetry books, *Crossing the Border* and *KORA: a story and eleven poems*. His writings have been published in numerous magazines and dailies; and his literary skills won him the first-ever 'Outlook-Picador Award for non-fiction' in 2001. Currently he is the General Secretary of Friends of Tibet, India, and has no permanent residence.

Tsering Wangmo Dhompa grew up in Dharamsala, India and Kathmandu, Nepal. She completed her BA and MA from Lady Shri Ram College, New Delhi, and received an MFA in Creative Writing from San Francisco State University. Tsering is the author of a book of poems, *Rules of the House* and two chapbooks, *In Writing the Names*, and *Recurring Gestures*. Tsering works for the American Himalayan Foundation and lives in San Francisco.

Tsamchoe Dolma did her schooling from Tibetan Children's Village school, Dharamshala and holds a bachelor's degree in science. She admires creativity, respects arts and loves writing. Tsamchoe works as a research assistant at Library of Tibetan Works and Archives and lives in Dharamshala.

Bhuchung D. Sonam was born in Chung Ri.bo.che, Tibet. He came to India in 1984 and studied in TCV school, Dharamshala. After graduating from St. Xavier's College, Ahmedabad, he received an MA in economics from M. S. University of Baroda. He worked for Paljor Publications,

New Delhi and his book of poetry *Dandelions of Tibet* was published in 2002. Currently he is a vagabond of low caliber. He can be reached at bdsonam@rediffmail.com

Thupten N. Chakrishar was born in 1980 at Ravangla, south Sikkim in India. He was educated in many different schools including Bahai Christian School, Tibetan Children's Village school Dharamsala and C.S.T Mussoorie. He was, perhaps, the first Tibetan high school student to write a fiction book in English *Anything for Tibet, My Beloved Country*. His poetry book, *Young Tibet* won the annual award for young poets from the International Society of Poets. Currently he is a graphic designer and the Creative Head of Young Tibet Designs, Youth Empowerment Initiative and the official graphic designer for His Holiness the 17th Gyalwa Karmapa. He is based in Delhi.

Namgyal Phuntsok Tsawa was born in December 1978 at Bodhgaya in Bihar. He graduated from Punjab University, India, and was editor of the Regional Tibetan Youth Congress's annual magazine. Currently he is General Secretary of National Democratic Party of Tibet. His first book, *The Call,'* was published in 2003 and the second book of poems, *The Silent Observer,* was released in May 2004. He lives in Dharamshala.

Tenzin Trinley studied in Tibetan Children's Village school, North India. His love of writing poems came after finishing school in 1994, with few years in Chandigarh and around different parts of India. Deeply concerned with the society and the environment he lives in, he writes to mirror his feelings and concerns from the heart. Currently he works as an English teacher and lives in Dharamshala.

Tenzin Gelek was born in Kollegal, South India. He finished his school from Central School for Tibetans, Mungod and did Computer Science from St. Aloysius College, Mangalore. Gelek currently works and lives in Bangalore.

Ugen Chophel was born at Patlikuhl, a tiny place in North India in 1977. He completed his schooling from Tibetan Children's Village school, Dharamshala, and worked as a contract teacher in TCV school Patlikuhl. Currently he lives in Chautra, Himachal Pradesh.

Kathup Tsering was born in Tsoe, a small town in Amdo, northeastern Tibet, where he was educated at a local high school. He escaped to India in 1994 after taking part in a demonstration demanding promotion of Tibetan culture and religion. In exile he joined Tibetan Children's Village school where he studied Tibetan and English. As the editor of bi-monthly Chinese Magazine, *The Soul of Snow* he translated many Chinese and English poems into Tibetan. Currently he is pursuing a BCA.

Index of the First Lines

'...... to Lithang and back, 56
A city there is which lone does stand, 2
A few stolen moments, 136
A few words to say, 161
A kiss immortalized in Kodak frame, 116
A man, 178
A poetic dilemma, alas! 76
A Tibetan *Geshe* came, 28
All set for the journey, 133
Along a dark tunnel I walk, 172
And if day was to dawn, 71
Another lonely night, 53
As skylarks hunt for their prey, 13
As the rain clouds gather in the sky, 64
As the stars fade in the morning sky, 63
Baba sells dreams at the steps of a *masjid*, 77
Before I fade away, 158
Behold thy eyes, 179
Born a village child, 44
Charity, the password for heavenly salvation, 49
Confusion, 26
Cry Tibet! My beloved Fatherland, Cry! 168
Darkness descends, 176
Death laughs in your eyes, 164
Denali – the mountain endowed, 32
Do not, 19
Don't be afraid, mother, 174
Emerging to the surface, 12
Exile, 20
For ages, 23
From home you have reached, 104
Gazing at twilight's splendour, 31
Grass was refusing to growth 101
He sits and gazes, with a song upon his lips, 63

Hello! And greetings, 58
Hide not your face, 81
Homer – the land gifted, 32
I am a terrorist, 112
I am just a soul in a fixed, 90
I am tired being on somebody else's land, 162
I am weary of this colourless wall, 78
I bare my breast to you, 69
I fall on the pavement, 163
I had a dream of a world so free, 180
I have no summer; no marigold, 61
I have seen many pictures, 87
I live in a paradise of my own, 160
I love you no less than my own self, 21
I met the snail queen yesterday, 130
I peel and peel and peel, 111
I sing for all things dead and alive, 147
I slowly gather up my shaggy herd, 65
I wait for freedom every month…every year, 173
I was promised a birth, 182
If I die my dear ones, 83
In case you forgot, 52
In my dreams I see three MIGs, 119
In the cave where silence reigns, 65
In the times now long forgotten, 5
Is it snowing in my motherland? 167
It is interesting this cacophony of words, 117
It mingles and mingles for toxic, 183
It's not a pledge made, 132
Its night again…., 125
Let me sing a song, 153
Let us not do for the glory, 89
Life's music, 51
Life delights, 88
Like a dry leaf, my heart crumbles, 159
Looking for cheap restaurants, 14

Loose ...gone down, 184
Made in China, 46
Morning, 35
M's mother was so beautiful, 97
My feet are wandering neath the alien star, 3
My life, 50
My thoughts, 42
My Tibet, 47
Now that our plough is broken, 67
Now that the dust has settled, 144
Oh! My friends, 155
Oh, you brave people, 68
om mani padme hum, 48
On the Friendship road, 142
On the right, a mountain with juniper trees—at its foot a, 11
Our tiled roof dripped, 103
Passing over the lofty mountains, 150
Poets everywhere are the same, 22
Read half a poem of Walt Whitman, 29
Reality and illusion, 86
She drew that tiny flower, 107
She is there at last, 122
She trotted down the muddy lane, 127
Sheep roam on the meadows, 18
Shy drizzles and a shimmering pond, 137
Silent souls swelled with feeling, 135
Since I lost the hiking trail, 39
Slowly and silently the sun peeps, 152
Solid Marpa, 7
Something inside me calls, 124
Sometimes you tell me, 74
Somewhere in that capital of Aryabhumi, 114
Starlit nights are here again, 169
Starry nights are here again, 170
Sun, 156
The beginner in meditation, 9

Index

The best minds of my generation are idiots, 10
The earth and sky held counsel one night, 1
The green, green field, 108
The head, 105
The Hostel Mess is closed, 109
The lonely heart is a ship, 23
The mist was gone somewhere in the depth of the valley, 138
The orange hue of filtered, 80
The raven caws, 55
The view from, 172
The wish of my Amala, 36
Their faces look the same –, 40
There are all-consuming shadows, 73
There are things in my mind, 75
There is no time to waste on you, 70
They are a dozen or more, 128
They were in full foliage, 143
This land of the teeming multitude, 149
Through my tainted glass, 140
Tibet is my destiny, 165
Torn between two countries, 45
We are all late, except him, 27
When the elder died in her sleep, 99
When my bamboo flute's, 34
With Mama's loving care, 84
World, so full of people, 139
Yes, Alaskans, we've driven enough plastic vehicles, 37
Yesterday, 57
Yet another day passes, 181
You are nothing but everything, 85
You eat with your right hand, 92
Zero! 43